OPEN LEARNING AND OPEN MANAGEMENT

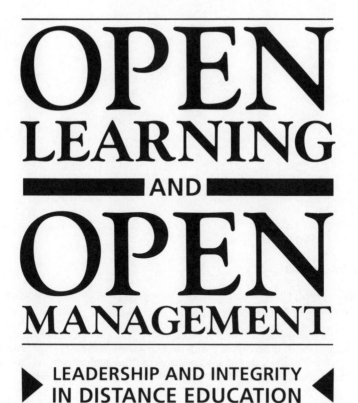

OPEN LEARNING

AND

OPEN MANAGEMENT

▶ **LEADERSHIP AND INTEGRITY IN DISTANCE EDUCATION** ◀

ROSS H PAUL

Kogan Page, London/Nichols Publishing, New York

First published in 1990 by Kogan Page Ltd
120 Pentonville Rd
London N1 9JN

British Library Cataloguing in Publication Data
A CIP catalogue record for this book is available from the British Library
ISBN 0-7494 0122-2
First published in the United States of America in 1990 by Nichols/ GP Publishing,
PO Box 96, New York, NY 10024

Typeset in 11/13pt Times by The Castlefield Press Ltd, Wellingborough, Northants
Printed and bound in Great Britain by Biddles Ltd, Guildford and King's Lynn

Library of Congress Cataloging-in-Publication Data
Paul, Ross H.
    Open Learning and Open Management: Leadership and Integrity in Distance
    Education / Ross H. Paul.
        p. cm.
    Includes bibliographical references.
    ISBN 0-89397-374-2; $39.50
        1. Distance education--Canada. 2. Adult education--Canada.
    3. Educational technology--Canada. 4. University extension--Canada--Case studies.
    I. Title.
    LC5808.C2P38 1991   90-7605
    378'.03--dc20   CIP

Table of Contents

Foreword
Myer Horowitz

I consider it an honour to take up Ross Paul's invitation and write a foreword for this book. I have known the author for more than 20 years, since he was one of my graduate students at McGill University. In this volume he reflects upon not only his relatively recent involvement at Athabasca University, one of the finest open-learning and distance-education universities, but also on his earlier experiences as a teacher and administrator in more traditional educational institutions.

Ross Paul set out to write a book about open learning and distance education. This he has done. In the process, however, he has developed important statements about learning and about management that will be useful for anyone interested in universities, in educational institutions at any level, and in bureaucratic organizations of various kinds.

Those of us who have served as educational administrators, especially during recent rather turbulent years, know how difficult it can be to focus beyond the issues and pressures of the moment. The very real daily concerns about funding, space, enrolments, programmes, bargaining and learner progress (to name just a few) can tax our energy and patience to their limits. Yet it is essential that we have a vision of where we must go if we are to serve our students and our colleagues. Usually, there are several ways of achieving the goals we set for ourselves, and while we have to be willing to alter our methods and procedures, we know that we must not do so at the expense of fundamental principles and values. Throughout, we must strive to be honest with the people with whom we relate, and, of course, we must be honest with ourselves.

That is an important leadership theme of Ross Paul's book, and it is that thrust which causes me to recommend it to students of administration and to practising administrators.

Myer Horowitz
Professor of Education
University of Alberta
March 1990

Preface

This book explores some of the experiences and issues I have faced in over 15 years of management at the senior levels in innovative, unconventional and often controversial institutions of higher education.

Dawson College, a sprawl of factories, apartment buildings, and period pieces (both buildings and faculty!) spread all over Montreal, was young, dynamic and chaotic during the time that I was there, dedicated as it was to process over product, to student parity and communal decision-making in the spirit of the late 1960s and early '70s. As the first CEGEP (*college d'enseignement general et professional*) for English-speaking students, it represented one of the first attempts by Quebec's anglophone minority to adapt a uniquely Quebecois institution to its own particular needs and culture. It grew rapidly from its foundation in 1969 until about 1975, and then held firmly at about 7000 full-time students.

Alberta's Athabasca University, an open university dedicated to extending access to a university education primarily via distance education, was described as a 'fly-by-night' organization by a friend who learned I was going there as its Vice-President Academic in 1980. Under threat of forced relocation north from Edmonton to Athabasca, it was tiny (all the staff could easily be assembled in a standard meeting room and the student body wasn't much larger), but everyone agreed it had great potential and held real promise for the future.

Both institutions have evolved considerably since I first joined – Dawson into a gigantic and much more conventional institution and Athabasca into a flourishing open university, seemingly less radical than in its early days, (though this is as much a result of other universities moving in its direction as of its own conservatism). While very different in character, both institutions have been seen as innovative, challenging the status quo and dedicated to extending access to higher education to those who might otherwise have missed out.

Both the college and the university have always had their detractors. As 'second chance' institutions, they have not benefited from the prestige that accrues so readily to more established, selective and elitist organizations. As innovative institutions, they have sometimes failed badly and more publicly than have their more conservative counterparts. As institutions which are 'different', they have often been misunderstood, misinterpreted and seriously underrated. These concerns notwithstanding, both have built an increasing legacy of strong supporters – the students who were given a chance by Dawson or Athabasca and who have taken advantage of this opportunity to succeed which would not otherwise have been available. This legacy has begun to have considerable impact not only on external perceptions of the institutions but on practices at the more conventional educational institutions. There can be no greater measures of Dawson's and Athabasca's achievements than the success of their graduates and the imitation of their practices by competitors.

Whatever their strengths and weaknesses, I have been up to my neck (and sometimes over my head) in their respective developments since 1973. This book represents a concerted attempt to step back from the excitement and achievements, from the stress and chaos, to relate and to apply that experience to the management of open learning in today's world – and in tomorrow's.

My Athabasca experience, which has been very results oriented, has caused me to care passionately about the achievement and impact of our ambitious but clearly delineated plans. However, there is still a large measure of the old Dawson in me, which means that I've really enjoyed the process of trying to figure out what we should do next and have always been committed to the notion that the way something is achieved is at least as important as the achievement itself.

My viewpoints have been tempered in some cases and reinforced in others by my experiences in Britain, as a teacher trainee in the PGCE course at the University of London in 1964–65 (where R S Peters so stimulated my interest in the authority of the teacher and in the work of Max Weber); as a doctoral candidate in Comparative Education at the University of London during the period 1971–73; as a Visiting Professor at the Open University during the spring of 1989; as participant in conferences in Cambridge, Chorley, Birmingham and Belfast; and as tourist and theatre buff on several other occasions.

In a recent article in the *Bulletin* of the International Council for Distance Education (ICDE)[1] I suggested a large number of similarities and only a few differences between the issues faced by open universities in the Canadian and British contexts. Among the similarities were the tremendous opportunities for open learning institutions in Britain,

Europe and, indeed, all around the world; the challenges not only of teaching but of managing 'at a distance' in providing regional support services to distance education students; the amount of travel and commuting done by people in the field; and the incredible growth in demand for and acceptance of open learning and distance education with the concomitant pressures on international bodies like the ICDE and Commonwealth of Learning. Such organizations are becoming major world forces in the coordination and dissemination of information, course materials and research in the development and delivery of distance education.

As the pioneer in distance education with the creation of the world's first major open university, Britain remains pre-eminent in the field. The Open University, National Extension College, Open College and Open Tech programmes are clear evidence of its strong commitment to open learning, notwithstanding the sometimes parochial nature of its debates about the differences between open learning and distance education (see Chapter 4).

The major difference which I have discerned between Athabasca University and the Open University, apart from the obvious one of scale of operation, is one central to this book: the extent to which one believes that an open university must be managed. While both countries share a common tradition of highly autonomous universities where academic freedom and tenure protect the integrity of research and scholarship and freedom of expression, there is a greater tendency in Canada to manage such institutions directly. This has particularly been the case for its open universities, while the irony is that, from my perspective at least, the Open University in Britain has been less open to modern concepts of management than have its much more established and traditional counterparts, Oxford and Cambridge. As I stated in the ICDE article:

> While this allows many of its excellent faculty and professionals to pursue their own interests and skills to the benefit of both the university and themselves, it leaves one wondering about more recalcitrant staff with whom no one seems to deal. From my perspective, at least, traditional universities in Britain are being forced to face such issues as performance indicators and individual accountability in a way that they never have before, and it is incumbent on the OU to develop its own processes before either the competition or the government force the issue in less palatable ways.[2]

With the recent appointment of John Daniel, a Canadian, as its new Vice-Chancellor, it will be interesting to see if attitudes towards and practices of management change appreciably in the next few years at the

Open University. Whatever the case, the Open University remains a strong leader in the field and I was most appreciative of the opportunity afforded by my visiting professorship.

I am grateful to Athabasca University for the seven-month leave of absence which enabled me to undertake this work. More importantly, I would like to recognize those who have helped me to put it together. Special thanks are extended to:

Ros Morpeth, for her enthusiasm and support every time I talked with her; **David Sewart,** for his support during my Visiting Professorship at the Open University in the Spring of '89; **Keith Harry** in England and **Lorin Hansen** in Canada for generous library support; and all those who read parts of the manuscript and offered constructive criticism, notably **Jane Brindley, Phyllis Frick, Margaret Haughey** and **Peter Holt.**

Ian Mugridge, a friend and colleague who wrestles with problems very similar to my own as Principal of the Open University of British Columbia who offered valuable advice and criticism.

I would also like to express my special appreciation to several people who have influenced me very significantly during my career:

Brian Holmes, Professor Emeritus of Comparative Education at the University of London, who taught me how to think critically;

Myer Horowitz, recently retired President of the University of Alberta and Chair of Educational Administration at McGill University when I was there in 1967–68 – everyone's favourite role model, including mine, who graciously consented to write the foreword to this book;

Squee Gordon, President of Humber College, Toronto, who gave me opportunity, self-confidence and the room to grow, and who taught me one of the most important lessons – the ability to laugh at oneself; and

Terry Morrison, President of Athabasca University, who has never stopped challenging almost all of my ideas and forced me to do the same.

Finally, the book is dedicated to David and Jonathan, my sons, who will have to face even more change than my generation has, and Jane Brindley, my wife, for her love, support and helpful criticism throughout this project.

Ross Paul
Edmonton
December, 1989

Notes

1. Paul, R H (1989), 'Impressions of a Visiting Professor', *Bulletin: International Council for Distance Education,* 21 (Sept). Milton Keynes: Open University, pp 49–53.
2. Ibid, p 50.

Part 1: Introduction

CHAPTER 1

'The Frog in Hot Water'

I'm a frog, you're a frog, kiss me (smack, smack),
And I'll turn into a prince, suddenly.[1]

While change may not always be as spectacular as a frog turning into a prince, neither is it always, or even usually, the product of carefully managed planning and logical incremental steps. While one might be able, with hindsight, to explain all of the factors associated with such dramatic changes as the rush of events in Eastern Europe which culminated with the opening of the Berlin Wall in November 1989, this does nothing reduce the startling impact of the news at the time it happens. In fact, even using the verb 'to culminate' represents restricted thinking which fails to recognize that even more dramatic events are probably just on the horizon and may have taken place between the time of writing and the publication of this book.

As an analogy with the difficulties we face in coping with change, we need not restrict ourselves to mythical frogs, for the real-life variety can apparently serve us just as usefully. According to Charles Handy, a frog will allow itself to be boiled alive in water that is heated slowly and steadily to the boiling point, because it is

> too comfortable with continuity to realize that continuous change at some point becomes discontinuous and demands a change in behaviour.[2]

While I sometimes wonder how scientists discover such things (and how many creatures were boiled before this particular characteristic of the frog was identified), Handy's analogy is one very appropriate to the challenge of leadership in a fast-changing and often discontinuous world. Change is exciting, challenging and rewarding, but it can also be threatening, alienating and frightening. Unfortunately, too many of us cope with change in the manner of Handy's frog.

Unlike Handy, most of us do not have the luxury of analysing what the frog should do from outside the pot. The real challenge is to be the frog and somehow assess what is happening and what responses are required, and then not only to communicate to all the other frogs what action they should take but also persuade them of this, even though many are very comfortable where they are, and, even more, help them to develop systems which enable them to jump out of the pot success-fully – getting out is one thing, where you land is quite another!

There are two lessons in this for the organizational leader. The first is to stress his or her responsibility to be alert and open to change; to seek it out and embrace it; to be willing to take risks; to be optimistic and flex-ible; and hence to provide leadership in forging new paths for the future. The second is to recognize that we are all like the frog, that we need help in recognizing and adjusting to change, that we can only cope with so much change at one time and that the process can be very stressful.

There has never been a more challenging or more important time for institutional leadership and good management. In a world of rapid change, technological innovation, and an unprecedented emphasis on new knowledge, it is increasingly difficult to retain overall perspective, to balance the necessity of change with our needs for peace, security and happiness. It is no longer enough to get a good education and, through training and experience, devote one's life to a particular job or series of closely related jobs.

Almost every social institution is undergoing challenge and change. Fewer and fewer families are conforming to the patterns of a few short years ago. It is more and more common for people to make dramatic career changes in mid-life. There are more and more women in the work force, and they are increasingly challenging men for the top jobs in organizations. As new technology finds ways to replace workers in menial jobs, there are concerns about unemployment, self-worth, and the use of unprecedented amounts of leisure time.

Much has been written about these changes and their impacts on people and organizations. Rather less has been written, however, about the importance of good management in ensuring that organizations are responsive to never-ending change. It is one thing to conduct good environmental scans (to assess external factors such as economic and demographic trends) and prepare effective strategic plans, and quite another to persuade others to implement these plans and to give them the support and tools with which to succeed. Management was never more difficult, never more rewarding, and never more important.

The book deals with a number of interacting and often opposing forces, themes which are central not only to the management of open-learning institutions but to any modern organization – dynamic change and yet the need for security; growth and restraint; interaction and inde-pendence; and centralization and decentralization.

The last of these, which I have confronted often in the management of Dawson's multicampus model and Athabasca's regional network, not only is one of the classic issues in management, but is particularly relevant to the evolution of my own country, Canada.

Canada has wrestled with this problem since its Confederation in 1867. Challenged throughout its history by the special needs of Quebec, a predominantly French-speaking province, Canada has 'muddled through' (following the British part of its heritage) but never really resolved the tensions between the legitimate demands of its quite diverse regions spread over one of the world's largest countries and its quest for a central identity, a strong defining culture, which can unite a scattered population.

In recent years, it has had both kinds of leadership. Pierre Trudeau, in power, with one brief interval, from 1968 to 1984, had a clear vision of a bilingual and bicultural Canada, one which depended on a strong central government to forge its identity. The charismatic Trudeau offered great hope to insecure Canadians and was never more popular than when he dealt effectively and boldly with terrorism in Quebec in 1970. However, in retrospect, his actions in invoking the War Measures Act to deal with a few small cells of activists while trampling on the human rights of many other people encountered more criticism. Similarly, his National Energy Policy, while beneficial to the central provinces of Ontario and Quebec which received oil at below world-market prices, alienated the western provinces which depended on oil revenues. It remains for history to judge Trudeau's era, but perhaps its best measure is the constitution – unlike any prime minister before him, Trudeau succeeded in repatriating the Canadian Constitution from Britain, but he did so without the agreement or signature of his own province of Quebec.

Trudeau has been replaced by a very different style of leader. Brian Mulroney, prime minister since 1984, is a compromiser who made his name as a mediator of labour disputes. His answer to the challenge of Quebec is the Meech Lake Accord, an 'accord' only in theory at the time of writing and one very much in danger of falling apart. His concept of a much more decentralized Canada may win more provincial support, but it could collapse if he fails at the same time to communicate a national vision, a *raison d'être* for the nation which transcends local interests, the vision of a whole that is greater than the sum of its parts.

Depending on one's political perspective, the two leaders can be described as either highly successful statesmen or disappointing failures. Trudeau generated more extreme reactions than does his conservative successor; both touched responsive chords in the Canadian population; but neither has thus far succeeded in resolving the Canadian dilemma. If Trudeau raised our hopes and aspirations in 1968, it is a far more cynical age 21 years later.

Perhaps the biggest concern as we move away from an era when our leaders were gods is that no one will lead, that events will increasingly happen serendipitously or randomly. The long-standing American distrust of 'too much government' was one which Ronald Reagan made the hallmark of his administration, and there are concerns that George Bush is similarly abrogating responsibility for leadership on many issues. This contrasts with Margaret Thatcher's success in Britain where the Iron Lady has been admired by many for saying what many others just thought and for doing when many others just dreamed. Nevertheless, time is apparently catching up with the strident Mrs Thatcher, as it does with almost all leaders, and the same personality traits that attracted many voters in earlier times are now undermining her credibility.

We apparently need different sorts of leaders at different times. Powerful individuals with a strong vision and the ability to communicate it can often induce or respond to major change much more effectively than can those with less obvious leadership qualities, but they may be less effective in managing the processes of coping with longer-term adjustments to the change. Mikhail Gorbachev's leadership has produced dramatic change throughout Eastern Europe, but it remains to be seen whether he is capable of coping with the forces which have thus been unleashed. Winston Churchill was the greatest of British heroes at the culmination of World War II in 1945, but the British people looked not to him but to Clement Atlee and the Labour Party when it came to picking up the pieces and rebuilding British society in the aftermath.

Returning to the Canadian context, the real tragedy would not be the bald fact of the separation of Quebec from the rest of the country but that such a separation took place because people just 'didn't care' until it was too late. In this case, it would be the rest of Canada who would be the 'frogs in hot water'. *Quelle ironie!* The biggest enemy of leadership and achievement is not opposition but apathy.

I do not believe that the leadership problems cited above are manifestations of a particularly poor crop of leaders. It is a reflection of the times, times when it is almost impossible for an individual to be 'on top' of everything that is going on, when there are strong lobby groups for all viewpoints and when there is less of a clear-cut morality to guide all actions. We know a lot more about our leaders these days – they are no longer hidden from us as caricatures, but are real people, warts and all. Ambiguity, information overload, and cynicism abound at a time when there was never a greater need for leadership. Ultimately, we get the leaders we deserve – the only ones who can legitimately complain about a lack of leadership are those who are at least willing to put themselves in positions of responsibility, and they are usually too busy defending their own actions to criticize those of others.

The particular case of the open university presents a fascinating microcosm of these issues, and one that has much to offer in informing the wider debates about leadership and social direction. In an age when so much is expected of education, there is already great concern about how poorly we train and educate our populace, especially as other societies, notably Japan, appear, to us at least, to be doing a much better job. At least in theory, an institution like an open university, dedicated to increasing access to higher education, to finding better ways to induce learning and promote the cause of lifelong learning, and to taking education and training to the people in their own time and in their own communities and workplaces, is one which should be in the forefront of social change and which should attract both attention and funding from government and the private sector.

Although formally a product of about the last 30 years, the open university is not a new idea, for its need was anticipated in a much earlier age, as Stuart Marriot discovered in an article published in *The University Extension Journal* in 1891:

> Before long some University will seize the unequalled opportunity . . . will boldly lay down a curriculum of study for degrees in new lines suited to the needs of those who desire to carry on their intellectual culture side by side with the regular business of life.[3]

While we have no way of knowing what time frame the author was working on, he would doubtless be disappointed to discover that it took until the mid-1960s, with the creation of Britain's Open University, for his ideas to be implemented on a grand scale.

Ideas of equality of opportunity have been around even longer (see pp 41–42 of Chapter 3), but the real challenge is to develop and manage institutions which make them a reality. The open university is very much this sort of institution, although its manifestation in almost every country has often fallen far short of its loftiest ideals.

Following the example of Britain's Open University, many Western countries established open universities aimed primarily at the adult student, many of whom pursued their education part-time while continuing as homemakers or in the work force. More recently, however, as John Daniel has documented,[4] distance education has so flourished in other parts of the world that there are an estimated three million post-secondary students in distance-education institutions in the USSR, China, South Korea and Thailand alone. Unlike their Western counterparts, most of these students are in the traditional college/university age range of 18–24, and most are studying full-time.[5]

While the open university means different things in different cultures and contexts, most such institutions closely resemble each other, and the frequent international conferences and the preponderance of journals and books on distance education and open learning attest to the value of shared perspectives on the problems and challenges that these relatively new institutions pose.

The interest here, however, goes beyond the microcosm of distance education and open learning. As knowledge institutions in a knowledge society; as institutions which combine highly specialized professionals with large production systems; and as organizations dedicated to the application of new information technologies to the business of teaching and learning, open universities also provide case studies of interest to those concerned with such universal issues as leadership, management and organization.

The theme of the book is that those responsible for the leadership and management of these institutions must emulate the principles they espouse in the performance of their day-to-day activities. Building on the 'value-driven' leadership approach advocated by Badaracco and Ellsworth,[6] the quest for open management is intended to ensure that the values of open learning drive all aspects of administration and decision-making in open universities.

While such value-systems are discussed throughout the book, it is up to each institution, through its long-range and strategic-planning operations, to define its own particular set, which will vary considerably from culture to culture and institution to institution. Nevertheless, it is perhaps appropriate that I declare my own particular orientations and biases at the outset.

The following assertions are central to my philosophy of education:

- That education is central to the development of a better life and a better world;
- That education is a never-ending process of discovery and self-discovery, learning, unlearning, and relearning;
- That most people can succeed in higher education, given the opportunity and support;
- That the goal of all formal learning systems is to assist people to become self-directed and independent learners so that they increasingly take responsibility for what they learn and how they learn it;
- That education is active, not passive, and that true learning leads to change and self-action (Friere's *praxis*);[7]
- That there are many ways to learn and to teach, that different people learn in different ways, and that the same people learn in different ways for different knowledge or tasks.

I offer a similar list pertaining to my philosophy of management:

- That leadership and management can make a difference;
- That there are many different ways to succeed as a manager;
- That the most important characteristics of a good leader are a clear vision of the future and the ability to articulate it and hence persuade others to pursue it and to achieve it;
- That openness, integrity, humanism and a sense of humour are essential components of good management;
- That, as important as achievement is in management, the way things are done is at least as important as what is done.

The rest of this book will explore these notions in the theories of open learning and in the practical experiences of trying to manage and lead innovative institutions of higher education over the past 15 years. In the process, all the idealism of my commitment to principles of open learning and open management will be challenged to the utmost – we shall see at the end how unscathed they emerge.

Notes

1. *The Frog Song* (Chevrier/Charlebois), sung by Quebecois singer Robert Charlebois and recorded for *1 fois 5,* Kebec Disc, 20 June, 1976.
2. Handy, C (1989), *The Age of Unreason,* London: Business Books, p 8.
3. Stuart Marriot (1981), *A Backstairs to a Degree: Demands for an Open University in Late Victorian England,* Leeds: Leeds Studies in Adult and Continuing Education, p 1.
4. Daniel, J S (1988), 'Distance Education and National Development' in Stewart, D and Daniel, J S (eds), *Developing Distance Education,* Oslo: ICDE, pp 21–30.
5. Ibid, p 27.
6. Badaracco, J L and Ellsworth, R R (1989), *Leadership and the Quest for Integrity,* Boston: Harvard School of Business.
7. Friere, Paulo (1970), *Pedagogy of the Oppressed,* New York: Continuum.

Part 2: The Management of Open Learning: Theoretical Perspectives

There are four chapters in this section, which sets both a theoretical framework and the context for the practical examples explored in Part 3.

Chapter 2 looks at the university as an organization, starting with the premise that its primary management challenge is the supervision of highly skilled professionals working in increasingly large and complex bureaucracies. It then goes on to review previous attempts to define organizational models for higher education. Each theory is found to be useful but also inadequate in portraying the entire context of higher educational organizations.

Building on this discussion, Chapter 3 introduces the open university, the context for the further exploration of the issues raised in Chapter 2. The philosophy of open learning and its evolution in various institutional forms are presented before Chapter 4 explores the professional – bureaucratic conflicts confronted by faculty members working in such institutions.

Chapter 5 introduces the concept of value-driven leadership as a response to the shortcomings of previous organizational approaches to higher education and suggests a theory of open management which is applied throughout the rest of the book.

CHAPTER 2

The Organization of Higher Education

Chapter synopsis

With reference to the pioneer work of Max Weber and Talcott Parsons, the author examines the growing phenomenon of professionals working in large organziations and the inherent conflicts between their client orientations and the hierarchical and impersonal norms of the bureaucracy. The implications of this conflict for those responsible for managing such professionals are set out and explored through several theoretical approaches to higher education – the bureaucratic, the collegial, the political and the anarchic. While each theory is found to be extremely useful and important, none is sufficient in itself as a complete model of the university as an organization.

The central dilemma: managing professionals in bureaucratic organizations

In earlier times, professionals worked alone or in loose collectives which preserved their autonomy and independence – doctors' clinics, lawyers' offices, research labs. However, over the past 50 years, and more recently with the advent of the 'knowledge' society and its emphasis on specialized expertise, more and more professionals have found themselves working in large bureaucratic organizations – research scientists in government or military agencies, teachers and professors in large schools and universities, doctors and nurses in large hospitals, and lawyers and accountants in big corporations.

While this employment has brought many benefits to these professionals, in the form of up-to-date capital equipment and research and development opportunities that only large organizations can afford to support, it has also challenged some professional norms previously taken for granted, and has created considerable conflict for both the practitioners and those who manage them.

There is a strong and well-documented basis of this inherent conflict between the client-orientated norms of the professional and the universalistic dimensions of a bureaucratic organization. For the latter, we turn to Max Weber.

Weber[1] is the father of modern organizational theory. His writings about the bureaucratic organization, based on what he termed legal-rational authority, are classic. The dimensions of his 'ideal-type' bureaucracy include hierarchical authority, formal rules and procedural specifications, specialized expertise, and impersonality (to ensure that everyone is treated equally and fairly).*

In the classic bureaucracy, each individual is located at a level of technical competence according to his or her expertise and degree of specialization. Jobs are defined specifically and quite narrowly to ensure that they are performed only by those with the requisite training and experience.

Increasingly, however, modern bureaucracies are staffed not just by technical experts but by fully qualified professionals who make strong claims to autonomy and self-direction. Talcott Parsons[2] was one of the first to notice and write about the rise of professionals in bureaucracies and to document the inherent contradictions between their role orientations and the dimensions of a bureaucracy.

Whereas the bureaucracy is founded on formal hierarchy (authority of office), impersonality, and formal rules and procedural specifications, a professional orientation emphasizes authority of person, and a strong personal client orientation which will frequently justify the breaking or bending of rules to suit the perceived needs of individual clients. The following table highlights the major similarities and differences between professional and bureaucratic role orientations:[3]

DIMENSION	PROFESSIONAL	BUREAUCRATIC
Authority	Personal, based on professional competence	Hierarchical, based on competence of office holder
Rules	According to professional judgement	Formal, written
Procedures	According to professional judgement	Formally specified
Client Treatment	Personal, specific to individual need as diagnosed by professional	Impersonal, objective, for equal treatment of all

*Weber's bureaucracy and its application to higher education are discussed on p 31–32 immediately below.

DIMENSION	PROFESSIONAL	BUREAUCRATIC
Technical Competence	Specialized education and training	Specialized education and training
Specialization	Emphasized for personal expertise	Emphasized for organizational expertise

It is interesting to note that both professionals and bureaucracies emphasize specialized technical competence, but whereas the rational organization of specialized office holders is the key to a successful bureaucracy, the professional relies on his or her specialized technical competence to gain and protect autonomy from the organization.

One of the biggest challenges for modern administration is the management of such professionals, a task usually carried out by fellow professionals who may or may not have training or experience in management. The potential for conflict is high:

- The professional's 'client' orientation clashes directly with the bureaucracy's emphasis on impersonality.
- The professional may want to bend rules to suit the needs of his or her particular client; the bureaucracy emphasizes formal rules and procedural specifications in an attempt to anticipate all possible situations and concerns. We all appreciate an understanding clerk who bends rules to recognize our particular circumstances, but we are also quick to cry 'foul'! when we perceive that someone else has been given special privileges or dealt with more quickly than we. We don't like people who 'play favourites' unless we are the ones benefiting from the favour.
- The professional makes diagnoses and prescriptions according to his or her expertise, whereas, in a bureaucracy, such decisions are usually made by superiors in the hierarchy.
- To the extent that the supervisor is not as professionally competent as the subordinate, the latter will resist the supervisor's authority in a manner inconsistent with the values of a bureaucratic organization. The typical solution to this is to hire as manager someone who is already a fellow professional. While this may increase the manager's ability to supervise, it may also result in a less interventionist model, given his or her respect for the autonomy of a professional colleague.
- Even if the manager is initially as professionally competent as anyone he or she supervises, it is extremely difficult for any person to maintain this competence while preoccupied with management issues. Universities attempt to cope with this by offering generous

leaves to those who have just completed a deanship or vice-presidency, but it is very difficult in fast-changing disciplines to 'catch up', and many who leave academia for administration never return to their disciplinary work.

One of the 'purest' examples of an institutional setting where these dilemmas are faced on a regular basis is the modern university. Henry Mintzberg classifies the university as a 'professional' organization where 'the members of the operating core exert a pull to *professionalize*, in order to minimize the influence that others, colleagues as well as line and technocratic administrations, have over their work.'[4] While Mintzberg himself admits that none of his organizational classifications exists in pure form and that any complex organization incorporates elements of the seven 'forces' which he has so far identified as acting on them,[5] it is contended here that the 'open' university rather more pointedly than most organizations incorporates two conflicting forces – the professional and the bureaucratic (Mintzberg's 'machine' category). In Mintzberg's terms, it is a professional organization with a significant machine organization embedded within it, with the interface between the two one of its most significant management challenges.

While Mintzberg's conception of a professional organization includes a 'machinelike' organization for the support staff who serve the professionals, in an open university, this bureaucratic component is far more prominent. Faculty autonomy is compromised by the course team concept and by the visibility of the course package (the teaching product). Such routinized functions as course production, the distribution of course materials and individualized student tracking and records systems impinge directly upon rather than merely support the teaching and learning process in the institution. Hence, open universities almost uniquely represent the strongest tendencies of both orientations – the professional autonomy of university academics and the bureaucratic demands of a large publishing house and service organization. The inherent conflicts between these orientations have major implications for how such institutions can be managed.

Before looking more closely at the management of open-learning institutions, it would be useful to review the theory of organizational models for higher education. In the process, reference will be made to ways in which universities have been governed and managed in the past to set the stage for later explorations of how this is having to change in the face of new pressures for diversification, role expansion, and public accountability.

Organizational models for higher education

While it is always an oversimplification to categorize, it is nevertheless useful to review the major models which have been suggested to explain how institutions of higher education are organized and managed. For purposes of this analysis, the following have been selected:

- the bureaucratic model;
- the collegial model;
- the political model;
- the anarchic model.

Each model will be reviewed, in turn, in terms of its contribution to our understanding of higher educational institutions but also with a view to identifying weaknesses of each in the eternal search for a better organizational model.

It should be acknowledged that the following analyses fall mainly within the 'functionalist' paradigm and that there have been other, more radical approaches to organizational theory. These have been very well portrayed by Burrell and Morgan,[6] who set up four quadrants around subjective/objective and regulation/radical change continua. This identifies four major paradigms – the functionalist (regulation/objective), interpretive (regulation/subjective), radical humanist (radical change/subjective), and radical structuralist (radical change/objective). While this is extremely useful in identifying the assumptions and limitations of any paradigm, notably functionalism, Burrell and Morgan's presentation can be criticized because it is an example of functionalism and hence undermines the very argument it is attempting to make.

THE BUREAUCRATIC MODEL IN HIGHER EDUCATION

Reference has already been made to Max Weber's ideal-type bureaucracy. Using that model as a methodological tool against which to measure a modern university, it is clear that universities exhibit many of the characteristics of bureaucratic organizations, a case advanced most notably by Stroup.[7]

Universities are usually divided up in hierarchical fashion, from the principal and vice-chancellor down through vice-presidents, deans and service managers, faculty and other professional and support staff. Employees hold offices, are paid fixed salaries, and are eligible for job security through tenure, while personal and organizational property are separated.

The bureaucratic model explains the operation of much of a modern university – its registry; its student services; the operation of its plant and facilities, library systems, and personnel and financial offices; its research infrastructure; and the organization and administration of the academic programme.

However, it is equally evident that the bureaucratic model is inappropriate to the major teaching and research functions of a university as well as to its policy development and governance. Perhaps most fundamentally, faculty claims to academic freedom and professional autonomy are direct challenges to the hierarchical authority of office which is the hallmark of the bureaucracy. The specialized technical competence which leads to a faculty member's original appointment is also the expertise which shields him or her from bureaucratic supervision. An academic's authority is derived not from the formal office but from his or her personal and professional education and expertise.

Kandel's distinction between the *interna* and *externa* of an organization is useful in this context.[8] The *interna* include all factors directly associated with the technical (teaching and research) function of the institution, while the *externa* are those administrative factors which support the *interna* (planning, budgeting, managing). Hierarchical bureaucratic systems are more appropriate for the *externa*, where line authority and system integration are important factors, but they are not conducive to the effective functioning of the *interna*. This has led many writers to suggest that, while the bureaucratic model explains much of the structure of a university, it is far less useful in understanding its processes.

In other words, it is very misleading to depict the functioning of a university with reference only to its formal organizational chart. Any attempt to understand university management and governance requires a model which looks more closely at the processes of planning and decision-making characterizing such organizations.

THE COLLEGIAL MODEL IN HIGHER EDUCATION

This concern led Millet[9] and others to analyse the university as a collegial organization, a loose collection of specialized professionals who seek consensus in decision-making while preserving the sacred autonomy of the individual professional in making decisions in the best interests of his or her client.

University governance is typically along collegial lines. Most major academic decisions must be made by a senate or academic council by vote of the member academics. Faculty are usually left to their own devices when it comes to research, teaching and evaluation of students, and any concerns about performance or standards tend to be dealt with in an open and collegial fashion.

This model has been very successful and is central to our conception of a university as an independent social body, one that is often critical of prevailing norms in its society and which is dedicated to the search for truth. Its foundation is the premise that claims to legitimacy are based on rigorous proofs – something is a fact because it can be shown to be one, through replication of its initial conditions, and not because someone higher in the hierarchy said it was so. Peer review, not hierarchical authority, determines legitimacy, and hence it is natural that a collegial structure has evolved to facilitate this process. This model is important in preserving integrity in research or in ensuring that faculty members are free to express unpopular political views or to challenge prevailing ways of doing things.

At the same time, the impact of collegiality has spread well beyond issues of scholastic integrity and academic freedom. Consensus is usually the preferred model for all sorts of decisions, from appointments to budget allocations, and an elaborate committee structure has usually evolved to facilitate this intention. In fact, of course, the decisions are seldom as collegial as intended, with both bureaucratic and political forces undermining the pure *collegium* advocated by the idealists.

As universities have become more complex institutions, competing with each other and with the private sector, learning to do more with fewer resources, and having to be much more fiscally accountable and responsible, the collegial model has been increasingly under attack and often abandoned or modified in times of crisis. This model is appropriate when there are common problems to be solved or when it is more important to get consensus and commitment than necessarily to find the most expeditious or cost-effective response to a particular concern. However, when quick decisions are necessary, when there are clear conflicts of interest between competing parties, or when unpopular decisions which are difficult to sell to the whole constituency are required, it is not a very effective way of trying to solve problems.

The author's experience with decision-making at Dawson College in Montreal offers an interesting illustration of this problem. The faculty of arts on one campus had evolved a very participatory and open process of decision-making which, while time-consuming and stressful, was central to the faculty members' conception of collegiality. Faculty positions were funded by an enrolment-driven formula, and, each year, the faculty met to divide up its overall share of resources among its various academic departments. This worked very effectively for several years – as academic dean, I assigned the faculty its formula-based staff allocation, and the faculty made the necessary assignments within that. However, the reason it worked was that student numbers were growing, and, hence, every year there was a bit more to hand out. The faculty was very proud of its ability to decide democratically and openly among competing bids until the year when enrolments dipped slightly and the amount to be awarded was slightly less than the previous year. After several hours of bickering, the faculty unanimously decided to throw the problem back to the academic dean and ask him to make the decision! A strong commitment to collegiality was quickly abandoned when the faculty members found out how divisive the cutting exercise was, and hence they referred it back to the academic dean, who could then be depicted as the common enemy by everyone.

A real challenge to traditions of collegiality has been the rise of faculty unions, which tend to be bureaucratic organizations intended to deal with the central administrative bureaucracy of an institution. They rely on formal rules and procedures to ensure that the administration plays no favourites, hence stressing the bureaucratic norm of impersonality.

Furthermore, there is a bureaucratization built right into the process of collective bargaining. After a first contract, which might be quite vague and general in some areas, both sides encounter cases not specifically covered by the agreement, and hence narrower and more specific clauses are introduced in the next round. This process, which repeats itself with each contract, tends to produce an agreement which is increasingly specific and rigid in interpretation and is thus less conducive to compromise and adaptability, and hence to collegiality.

This evolution is mirrored in the development of faculty associations and unions, which tend to increase in size and complexity as the full impact of workloads and responsibility for collective bargaining is realized. In order to compete effectively with administrations, which usually have access to more resources, the unions evolve from loose collectives to increasingly bureaucratic organizations, complete with hierarchies, committees, legal support, and formal rules and regulations. In cases where locals are affiliates of large central unions, this bureaucratization is even more evident, and faculty members may feel a loss of control over their own association.

While expressing his sympathy with the events and conditions which have led to the rise of collective bargaining in universities, Millet concludes that faculty members have as much to lose as to gain from this more confrontational style of decision-making, and he concedes that it constitutes a direct threat to the collegial relationships which he advocates for a university.[10] The process, of necessity, draws a clear distinction between faculty and management and thus undermines the whole basis of collegiality.

Given the inadequacy of the collegial model in representing the full complexity of a modern university, university leaders have increasingly looked to other models of governance and decision-making (see pp 35–8 on 'political', and 'anarchic' models). However, it is certainly premature to write off the importance of collegiality in university management and governance, as many aspiring or short-term presidents have found out. Interestingly enough, a number of observers, notably the British organizational theorist Charles Handy,[11] are advising private-sector organizations to pay a lot more attention to university models of collegial governance as businesses increasingly face the challenges of managing specialist professionals in order to maintain their own competitive advantages in the marketplace. The characteristics of university management which may be most appropriate include:

- an emphasis on 'leadership' rather than 'management';
- delegation to highly qualified specialists with concomitant freedom from hierarchical interference;
- strong commitment to ongoing professional development;
- strong emphasis on research and development;
- collegial decision-making in certain areas of specialist technical competence.

In short, although inadequate to represent the organizational structure of a modern university, the collegial model is integral to its management and governance because it best lends itself to professional, as opposed to administrative, authority.

THE POLITICAL MODEL IN HIGHER EDUCATION

J Victor Baldridge[12] was dissatisfied with either of the above models. Without denying their importance and fundamental place in a modern university, Baldridge found that neither was very useful in explaining how decisions were made in the universities with which he was familiar. The bureaucratic model was weak in dealing with 'non-formal' forms of power and in its emphasis on structure over process. While aimed more at the processes of decision-making, the *collegium* approach and its emphasis on consensus failed to explain or deal with conflict. For Baldridge, writings by Millet and others were more normative than descriptive, overlooking what 'is' in favour of their view of 'what ought to be'.[13]

He thus borrowed from sociology and political science in proposing a political model of decision-making, one which recognized the predominance of power groups. Citing conflict theory (Coser, Dahrendorf), community-power theory (Hunter, Dahl), and an informal-groups approach (Selznick), Baldridge's political model focuses on policy formulation by analysing factors of the social context, identifying how interest groups articulate and advance their causes, how these feed into the legislative process, and hence how policy is developed and executed. Baldridge applied his model in a study of New York University, and it is relevant to note the volatility of events on American campuses at the time of his research (1968), when both students and faculty were strongly challenging the traditional power of university administrations and boards of trustees.

There is no question about the usefulness of Baldridge's model in analysing and understanding much of what goes on in a modern university. Especially since the volatility surrounding campus governance in the late 1960s and early '70s and the consequent rise of unions on campus, universities have been overtly political institutions. More recently, pressures for accountability and productivity have introduced new and stronger shareholders, notably government and industry, so that funding is increasingly earmarked to specific ends, and traditional norms of collegiality and autonomy have been confronted directly by those who provide most of the institution's resource base.

At the same time, the political approach suffers from the same limitations as the bureaucratic and collegial models in that it explains only part of a university's functioning and is effective only when combined with them to address both structure and process in university governance. Even then, however, theorists have not been particularly successful in predicting or explaining events on campus. This quest for a scientific approach to such complex matters has been somewhat debunked by another viewpoint, the 'anarchic' approach suggested by Cohen and March.

THE ANARCHIC MODEL IN HIGHER EDUCATION

One of the most appealing approaches for those who have tried to manage universities is Cohen and March's[14] 'anarchic' model, one which preceded and anticipated the broadly popular book on management, Peters and Waterman's *In Search of Excellence*.[15] While it sometimes reads more like satire than scholarship, Cohen and March's book is a serious analysis of the modern university, which they depict as an 'organized anarchy'. For them, before one can discuss principles of management and leadership in a university, it is critical to recognize that the university's goals are vague and diffuse, its technology unclear (they suggest that universities do not understand their own processes), and its participation fluid (individuals pick and choose their issues, and it is not always easy to predict which one will become a *cause célèbre* at any given time).[16]

> Although a college or university operates within the metaphor of the political system or a hierarchical bureaucracy, the actual operation of either is considerably attenuated by the ambiguity of college goals, by the lack of clarity in educational technology and by the transient character of many participants.[17]

These ambiguities and uncertainties render traditional forms of management meaningless or impotent. The authors challenge rational theories of choice which presume pre-existent goals in such rapidly changing times. In advocating 'sensible foolishness' and 'playfulness', they underline the difficulties faced by today's university president in dealing with the many interest groups, hidden agendas and natural inertia of the prevailing social structure. In examining such important regular decision-making challenges as planning the budget, developing educational policy, and ruling on academic tenure and planning, Cohen and March demonstrate considerable insight and imagination in suggesting how one can lead in such an ambiguous environment. They suggest that goals should be treated as hypotheses, intuition as real, hypocrisy as transition, memory as an enemy and experience as theory.[18]

No one with experience in university governance can deny the validity of much of what Cohen and March have to offer. Plans take on new rationales after the fact, presidents look good in good times and bad in bad times, and subtle differences in timing can have drastically different impacts on what decisions are made. Their writing has appeal primarily because it is grounded in experience and because it doesn't see leadership merely in legal – rational terms. Hence, the expectations for a university president are somewhat reduced, and he or she should be less self-flagellating if the institution doesn't end up quite as intended. The ideal incumbent will somehow find an appropriate and sustaining balance between foolishness and rationality.

While their analysis adds considerably to the earlier models cited, it does not replace them. In response to Cohen and March, Millet takes issue with their initial premises, suggesting that they have failed to distinguish between the overall direction of the university and problems of priority within the faculties.[19]

> The organized anarchy observed by Cohen and March was not so much the organized anarchy of the university as it was the organized anarchy of the faculty profession within the university.[20]

He suggests that the faculty, not the president, are the managers of learning and denies that the goals of the university are not clear – it is the priorities and methodologies within the overall goals that lead to conflict.[21] Hence, there is usually general agreement on the overall objectives of the institution, provided they are not made too specific or operational, but such institutions are well known for the difficulties they face in soliciting any sort of consensus as to how such objectives are to be achieved. It is perhaps not surprising that, as individuals recruited for their independent minds and raised in a climate of academic freedom, faculty members find it so difficult to agree on anything but this recognition does not make the academic sector any easier to manage.

In a sense, then, Millet and Cohen and March are focusing primarily on the management of the academic sector and of faculty governance. The modern university is a much more complex institution of which this is only one, albeit the key, part, and hence neither the collegial nor organized-anarchy model is a completely satisfactory representation. Furthermore, pressures for more accountability, for diversification of funding, and for opportunity for younger academics during periods of retrenchment, have challenged collegial modes of decision-making, especially where they have been perceived as too slow or cumbersome in responding to an ever-changing environment.

Mintzberg also takes issue with Cohen and March's notion of professional organizations as 'organized anarchies'.[22] He examines the various sorts of strategic decisions and defines three categories – those made by professional judgement, usually by individuals within the norms of their profession; those made by administrative fiat, especially those affecting financial decisions or the organization of basic support services; and those made by collective choice, including the creation of programmes and departments, hiring and promotion decisions and the development of budgets.

For Mintzberg, neither the collegial nor the political model of decision-making is, in itself, adequate to govern or explain decision-making in a professional organization. Instead, he focuses on strategies, adding 'analysis' to the 'garbage can' decision-making model contained in March and Cohen's organized anarchy, noting that

> the important collective decisions of the professional organization seem to be most influenced by collegial and political processes, with garbage can pressures encouraging a kind of haphazardness on one side (especially for less important decisions) and analytical interventions on the other side encouraging a certain rationality (serving as an invisible hand to keep the lid on the garbage can, so to speak!)[23]

The challenge is to find an approach to leadership which will benefit from the insights derived from the four approaches to the organization of higher education discussed above. Before addressing this issue, however, it is important to locate it in the context of open learning and distance education, an issue that is addressed in Chapter 3.

Notes

1. Weber, M (1947), *The Theory of Social and Economic Organizations*,

trans Henderson A M and Parsons T; ed with intro Parsons, New York: Oxford University Press.

2. Parsons, T (1951), *The Social System,* Glencoe, Illinois: Free Press, pp 428–79.
3. Adapted from Robinson, N (1967), 'Teacher Professionalism and Bureaucracy in School Organizations', *Canadian Education and Research Digest,* VII (March), pp 29–46.
4. Mintzberg, H (1989), *Mintzberg on Management: Inside Our Strange World of Organizations,* New York: Free Press, p 112.
5. Ibid, p 257.
6. See, for example, Burrell, G and Morgan, G (1979), *Sociological Paradigms and Organisational Analysis,* London: Heinemann.
7. Stroup, H (1966), *Bureaucracy in Higher Education,* New York: Free Press.
8. Kandel, I L (1933), *Comparative Education,* Cambridge, Mass.: Riverside Press, pp 216–17.
9. Millet, J D (1962), *The Academic Community: An Essay on Organization,* New York: McGraw-Hill.
10. Millet, J D (1980), *Management, Governance and Leadership: A Guide for College and University Administrators,* New York: Amacom, pp ix, x.
11. Handy, C (1989), *The Age of Unreason,* London: Business Books, p 113.
12. Baldridge, J V (1971), *Power and Conflict in the University: Research in the Sociology of Complex Organizations,* New York: John Wiley and Sons.
13. Ibid, p 14.
14. Cohen, M D and March, J G (1974), *Leadership and Ambiguity,* New York: McGraw-Hill.
15. Peters, T and Waterman, R H (1984), *In Search of Excellence: Lessons from America's Best-Run Companies,* New York: Harper & Row.
16. Cohen and March, op cit, p 3.
17. Ibid, p 83.
18. Ibid, p 226.
19. Millet, op cit, 1980, p 184.
20. Ibid, p 199.
21. Ibid, p 184.
22. Mintzberg, op cit, p 182.
23. Ibid, p 187.

CHAPTER 3

Open Universities – the Test of All Models

Chapter synopsis

Open universities are cited as useful test cases for exploration and development of organizational models in understanding the management of professionals in large bureaucracies. In this chapter, the concepts of open learning and distance education are explored and defined, with a view to developing a values system which will drive the leadership model described immediately above. In Chapter 5, which follows, this model will then be tested against a number of typical practical dilemmas faced by managers of open-learning systems.

The philosophy of open learning

Open learning is an elusive term, meaning many different things to different people (see 'A Night at the Pub' immediately below). In the most general sense, it is a relative term, referring to degrees of openness compared to some existing practice. Hence, an open-admissions policy is one which places few or no restrictions on entry, in contrast to those applying strict selection criteria.

In practice, no educational institution is completely open, for an institution on the absolute open end on all dimensions of a closed – open continuum would not be an institution at all. Instead, one would have achieved the complete 'deschooling' advocated by Ivan Illich.[1]

Nevertheless, the history of education and, most recently, of higher education, has seen a strong trend towards a philosophy of 'more open' learning. Fletcher's description[2] of the evolution of the modern university provides a useful overview of why this has come about.

He traces the evolution of Oxford and Cambridge, with their emphasis on the collegiate system, to earlier monasteries where 'groups of scholars committed to a love of scholarship in the setting of a community life' were assembled.[3] The twelfth-century Italian Cathedral

Schools introduced the notion of self-government and professional education, the seventeenth century brought research, and the nineteenth saw the development of teacher-training and technical universities and colleges.[4]

In his classic, *A Cultural History of Western Education,* R Freeman Butts[5] traces the social and intellectual roots of our modern educational system. The value of education for the liberation, enlightenment and equality of all people can be traced from Plato and Aristotle, through the social humanitarianism of Rousseau and the Encyclopaedists in France, to Jefferson, Mann and Dewey in the USA.

It is the twentieth century, however, which has seen strong movement towards the expansion and democratization of higher education. Many of the factors in this trend, according to Fletcher,[6] have had more to do with pragmatism and economic development than social altruism and idealism.

It has been only since about 1900 that economists have been interested in the relationship between economic investment and economic progress, finding that 'return from investment in education is much higher than was generally supposed'.[7] This lesson was learned in the first half of the century through the rapid expansion of secondary education, and there are few, if any, governments which do not accept a fundamental relationship between investment in education and economic return. Other economic forces which have had an impact on the expansion of higher education have been the rise of the professions and new technology which combine to make demands for new, highly trained specialists and better researchers.

Major powers have also seen higher education as a crucial factor in nation building, both in terms of seeking international competitive advantage and enhancing military power, which has emphasized science and technology, and of developing foreign-service and diplomatic corps, which has encouraged such disciplines as history, economics, languages, political science and sociology. The apparent relationship between investment in higher education and economic and political success has encouraged developing countries to follow suit.

The opening up of higher education has not been exclusively for such utilitarian purposes, however. Nineteenth-century egalitarianism was the first to break down the exclusiveness of admission to higher education,[8] and the twentieth century has seen unmistakable trends towards the democratization of education, so that universal primary and secondary education is a reality in most countries, and the proportion of the population attending higher-educational institutions is growing steadily almost everywhere.

Open learning is merely one of the most recent manifestations of a gradual trend towards the democratization of education. The use of the term 'open' admits that education and learning have traditionally been 'closed' by various barriers – entrance requirements, time constraints, financial demands, geographical distances, and, much more subtly, social and cultural barriers, as well as those of gender.

An open-learning institution is one dedicated to helping individuals overcome these barriers to their further education. Our primary interest here is in open universities, institutions which provide open admission to adult students and, through flexible policies and a variety of delivery mechanisms, notably distance education, provide access to and success in university education to those previously denied such opportunity.

The institutions known as 'open universities' vary considerably in form and structure, and some are more open than others. Their common characteristics are the following:

- A commitment to the belief that most adult students, regardless of age, gender, economic status, geographic location, employment status, and previous educational experience, given the opportunity and support, can succeed in studies at the university level.
- A concomitant commitment to providing structures, processes and services which assist such students in overcoming these various barriers to university access and support.
- At the risk of circular reasoning, we can say that open universities are most obviously those institutions which choose to define themselves in that way. It does not necessarily follow that they are more open on any specific dimension than any other institution, but this definition simply indicates that a commitment to the dimensions of open learning suggested immediately above is fundamental and central to their *raison d'être*.

There are enough loopholes and ambiguities in this discussion already to suggest that terms like 'open learning', 'distance education' and 'open-learning institution' may be more elusive than first meets the eye. Before this matter is pursued further, the reader is invited to eavesdrop on a recent pub conversation.

What is open learning anyway? A night at the pub

Especially in the United Kingdom, where the proliferation of 'open' institutions (National Extension College, Open University, Open College and, most recently, Open Poly) has spawned an extremely competitive atmosphere as different organizations scramble to take advantage of government-funding schemes, there is a strong and ongoing debate about what 'open' really means and about differences among such concepts as open learning, distance education and flexible learning.

There has been no end of attempts to define these terms clearly, the most recent and thorough being that by Greville Rumble.[9] It is in the spirit of accepting his emphasis on the importance of language that the following is offered. It borrows extensively from Rumble and from Roger Lewis.[10]

The author was fortunate enough to receive a transcript of the following conversation which took place in a pub on the outskirts of Milton Keynes during a recent conference on open learning.* The principal participants are:

Dr Derek Bludgeon, a senior manager from the Open University;
Dr Felicity Facey, an educational theorist who tutors for the Open College;
Sir Cyril Cynic, a retired vice-chancellor from an Australian 'dual-mode' university.

Facey and Bludgeon are sitting in a corner in earnest conversation. Cynic is standing at the bar, working on his third Scotch.

Facey: I'm tired of all the prominence given to distance education, just because that's what the Open University claims to be doing. Distance education is a glorified term for correspondence education, an admirable attempt to deliver education to remote learners but an educational experience which tends to be narrow in focus and which makes little provision for interaction, debate or ambiguity. Open learning, on the other hand, is not remote at all, but an interactive process where the student is open to pursue various options in his or her own time.

Bludgeon: With great respect (*Bludgeon always says this when he means 'without much respect'*), Dr Facey, you've created a false continuum. Distance education and open learning are not opposites but different concepts. You've confused the ends with the means. Open learning is a concept whereby the student is in control of his or her own learning, while distance education is merely one means by which open learning can be achieved.

Facey: I don't see what distance education necessarily has to do with open learning. It may make learning more open than it would have been had the student had no access whatsoever to formal education, but, otherwise, distance-education systems could be as 'closed' as any

---

*It should quickly be obvious to the discerning reader that any conversation among three academics which ends so quickly in near unanimity can be only a work of fiction.

conventional ones if all they do is disseminate knowledge via a printed package.

Bludgeon: You are missing the point entirely. There is no real difference between the Open College's 'open' learning and the Open University's 'distance education'. You want to distance yourself from distance education because you're worried about being swallowed up by the OU.

Facey: I should think it might soon be the other way round. Anyway, the point is not what the two institutions do but what they call what they are doing. Where there are similarities between our modes of operation, they are derived from our mutual commitment to open learning, not because open learning and distance education mean the same thing.

Cynic: (*who has been drawn into the conversation for lack of money for another Scotch*) What, are you two arguing about the differences between distance education and open learning? What a waste of bloody time! I don't see the point in trying to make a distinction.

Bludgeon: (*interrupting*) It's about as useful as the Australian preoccupation with debating the merits of single- and dual-mode institutions

Cynic: (*ignoring the jibe*) Why don't we just get on with running our institutions properly and stop these word games that don't mean anything to anyone anyway?

Bludgeon: But that's where you're wrong! It is very important that we are clear on these terms. If we label all these very different approaches to teaching, training and learning as 'open', we are misusing the term badly. What is worse, we may be deluding ourselves into thinking that we are providing open learning when, in fact, the system is quite closed.

Cynic: I see your point. My impression of this country is that you can get government funding just because you call your institution or project 'open' something.

Bludgeon: (*laughing*) Not any more! Not after Maggie got burned for so publicly supporting the Open College.

Facey: Don't be so quick to count us out. We're very much the wave of the future, working hand in hand with industry to develop education and training to their highest levels.

Bludgeon: The corporate training approach which the Open College is now taking is open only to company employees who are sponsored by their employers. What's so open about that?

Facey: And I suppose that having to wait 18 months to take a paced course is any more open? If the Open University is so open, how come it hasn't done more to democratize education; to attract the working classes, more women or ethnic minorities?

Cynic: Hold it, you two. If we must have this ridiculous discussion, let's at least refrain from shooting each other. You're both right and you're both wrong. Both the Open College and the Open University are open in some ways and closed in others. In both cases, they're more open than most of the conventional alternatives and surely that's the point. 'Open' is a relative term.

Bludgeon: Yeah, like grandmother or grandfather. But you're right – it's not just an OU/OC dispute. I agree with Roger Lewis's model of open learning which sees it as a sort of ideal-type against which any given system can be measured.

Facey: Oops, I agree, too. It must be a relative term because few of us would advocate a completely open learning system. A completely open system would not be a system at all – an individual would decide to learn something in his or her own way, time, and place, and he or she would decide when the learning activity was over and how valuable it had been. We don't need institutions for that, as Ivan Illich used to remind us.

Cynic: (*bored and hoping to steer the argument to quick resolution so that one or other of his colleagues can stand him another Scotch*) I'm still not sure I understand the value of all this, but may I suggest that we are in agreement with the following postulates:

(1) There is no such thing as a completely open learning system. Instead, we can assess the relative openness of a given institution on such considerations as accessibility, flexibility, and student control over learning outcomes.

(2) Distance education is one means of opening up educational opportunity to students who might not otherwise have it. Again, however, it is not a single concept – most so-called 'distance- education' systems involve some face-to-face or technologically interactive delivery.

(3) Distance education is thus a means to the end of open learning. Open learning is any system which removes the barriers that are preventing the student from learning.

(4) None of our institutions represents a truly open learning environment. Every one of them is compromised in one way or another; some by intention but most by the inevitable conservatism and bureaucratization of function that characterize all universities.

(5) All this notwithstanding, we should be damned proud of our open institutions. They have opened up more doors and given more confidence to more people who would never otherwise have pursued a formal education. There are people all over Britain, and increasingly all over the world, who are grateful for the opportunities which our open educational institutions have offered. In fact, there may be a few in this pub. If we can find them and then identify ourselves, they might demonstrate their gratitude by standing us each a round or two. What do you say?

Facey and Bludgeon: (*together*) I'll drink to that!

Bystander: (*shuffling up to the group a bit timorously*) I say, I hope you don't mind, but I couldn't help overhearing your chat about distance education. Tell me, I've always wondered, is distance education a discipline?

Publican: (*ringing bell very loudly*) Time, ladies and gentlemen, PLEASE!

Dimensions of openness

While this is a book about management, it is in the context of 'open learning', a commitment to the fundamental values cited below. The literature and current debate suggest considerable confusion among a number of similar terms, including open learning, distance education and flexible learning.

A major variable in a model of 'openness 'is the extent to which the learner controls the educational process – its content, how it is learned (organization of materials, various media and teaching methods), where it is learned (home, regional centre, on campus), when it is learned (start dates, self- or institutionally paced) and whether and how it is assessed.

For purposes of this book, open learning is depicted as an ideal-type, a construct which incorporates a number of fundamental values. From this perspective, almost no formalized provision of education will reach the ideal on all the continua suggested, for, as Facey suggested above, the extreme would not be an institution at all but some form of what Ivan Illich envisioned in his *Deschooling Society*.[11] The point is not so much whether or not a particular educational system can be classified as 'open' but whether it is more open than a previous alternative on the following dimensions.

ACCESSIBILITY

Open learning is characterized by a commitment to helping students, especially adults, overcome such traditional barriers to a postsecondary education as:

Prior academic credentials. Open learning means a commitment to open admissions, a belief that most adult students lacking formal qualifications can succeed in university-level studies if given the (or another) opportunity. They are admitted on a 'first come, first served' basis, limited only by the availability of the appropriate programme or of course places (usually governed by availability of course materials or staff rather than physical space).

Time. Many adult students, because of work and/or family respon-sibilities, cannot manage the full-time (usually also 'day' time) commit-ment that most degree programmes require. Open learning includes a commitment to helping the student to find ways to study in his or her own time.

Physical location. In open learning, the institution comes to the student rather than vice-versa, and thus provides access to those located in com-munities not otherwise served by formal educational institutions. This is usually provided through printed study materials prepared especially for home study with the support of a great variety of media and services, including tutoring by correspondence, telephone or teleconferencing, and using such information technologies as computer-assisted learning, interactive video-disc and satellite television.

Financial constraints. By allowing students to study in their own time and place, and on a full- or part-time basis, open learning assists them to overcome financial barriers to formal education by allowing them to study while holding a full-time job or raising a family. It may also provide the requisite study materials more cheaply than would normally be the case.

Personal characteristics. An area that has not received as much attention in this sort of analysis is the collection of barriers to learning erected by the students themselves. The argument here is that a true commitment to open learning takes these into account, and much of this book focuses on this area. Too often, adult students tend to blame themselves rather than the institution for their failures, and this presents a formidable challenge to the latter in helping students overcome their insecurities and deficiencies, a challenge that must be met if the open door is to be more than a revolving one.

Social responsibility. Such institutions usually have a deliberate orienta-tion towards the traditionally disadvantaged – those from lower socio-economic strata or aboriginal groups, prison inmates and others tradi-tionally denied places at a university. As with so many other attempts to provide for a more open society, however, this element of openness is often less prevalent than is admitted, and research almost inevitably demonstrates that the proportion of students from disadvantaged strata is significantly below that held out for such institutions at the time of their inception.[12]

FLEXIBILITY

Institutionalized flexibility is an integral part of an open learning system, but it is a more fundamental issue than simply increasing accessibility. It stems from a strong commitment to the learner as the starting point for all learning.

In the traditional institution, the main task of the administrator is to ensure that the right learner is in the right classroom at the right time with the right professor. What happens then is left up to the latter (and only sometimes to the student). In a truly open learning institution, these factors are governed much more directly by the student, who has far more control over the learning environment than is usually the case. In practice, however, this may also be a bit of an illusion. Writing in the context of Britain's Open University, David Harris cautions against this common assumption:

> Despite the promise of a radical departure from existing practice, in the name of liberating the learner, there is a risk of merely modernising existing practice and subjecting the learner to more rational and individualised controls.[13]

Among the characteristics of institutions which are more open, then, are:

Frequent admission periods. Instead of two or three semesters a year scheduled primarily for the convenience of the organization of classes, students may be able to start courses individually and more frequently, say, at the beginning of any month.

Self-pacing. Students may frequently be able to work at their own rates (within a predetermined time period), submitting essays and papers according to their own schedules and writing examinations when they feel ready for them (rather than when the institution schedules them).

Optional support services. The institution attempts to provide a broad range of student-support services, including tutoring, counselling and advising, but it is left up to the individual whether or not he or she takes advantage of these.

LEARNER CONTROL OVER CONTENT AND STRUCTURE

In the optimum case, the student is able to negotiate what he or she wishes to learn on an individual basis. The student is also able to determine the order in which various topics are approached, and how he or she is to be assessed. Typically, so-called open-learning institutions have been far more conservative in these areas than they have been in providing accessibility and flexibility in modes of course delivery, as they have depended on control of curricula, evaluation and accreditation for their academic credibility.

CHOICE OF DELIVERY SYSTEMS

In the optimum open-learning institution, the student has maximum ability to choose delivery systems and learning processes most appropriate to his or her individual requirements. Not everyone learns the same way, and the same person learns in different ways under different circumstances or for different subject matter. A challenge for all educational institutions, the matching of delivery systems to individual learning needs and styles is a particular problem for distance-learning institutions, especially as it is not particularly well addressed by the prevailing behaviourist or educational-technology approaches to course development.[14]

ACCREDITATION

One of the strongest barriers to openness is the emphasis placed on quality and accreditation by universities and colleges. Morrison[15] notes that much of the supposed concern with quality which underpins the accreditation system has more to do with exclusion, selection and tracking. It follows that the most open institution would not offer credit courses. However, given that the overwhelming context for post-secondary education is within the credit system, degrees of openness can be measured in terms of:

- the recognition of courses accredited by other institutions for transfer credit;
- the right of students to 'challenge' for course credit through special examinations designed for that purpose;
- provision for 'experiential learning', the granting of credit on the basis of an assessment of the individual's life experiences.

CONCLUSION: THE GAP BETWEEN PROMISE AND REALITY

As values central to the concept of open learning, the above concepts should drive all decision-making and priority-setting within open-learning institutions. However, as is discussed throughout this book, the process of implementation is one that frequently threatens this commitment, and no institution comes near matching the ideal type on all dimensions.

By and large, then, institutions claiming to be open are simply more open than their more conventional counterparts on specified and sometimes quite limited dimensions of openness. Lewis has done a useful job of illustrating this,[16] and Rumble has forced the question of the relative importance of one or more dimensions, notably access.[17]

The British preoccupation with the debate about open learning and distance education, which has received a lot of attention in recent editions of *Open Learning* and in several new textbooks,[18] has strong political connotations in that country, but it has also usefully focused more attention on our use of these terms in other applications. Its usefulness has been primarily to challenge justifiable pride in what open-learning institutions have achieved to date and to force those of us employed in them to identify significant gaps between theory and practice, and hence to suggest ways in which they could be much more open.

Definitions

For purposes of this book, 'open learning' is an ideal-type construct against which various institutions can be measured (see the dimensions set out above). It is not an absolute concept which distinguishes some institutions from others, although, as Rumble has observed, many have successfully promoted themselves as such in order to capitalize on government funding and support for such institutions.[19]

'Distance education' is one means towards the end of open learning. It describes noncontiguous learning whereby the learning process takes place 'away' from the institution, although, again, it is not an absolute term. Escotet's statement, cited in Rumble,[20] provides a good summary of this position:

> *Open education* is particularly characterized by the removal of restrictions, exclusions and privileges; by the accreditation of students' previous experience; by the flexibility of the management of the time variable; and by substantial changes in the traditional relationships between professors and students. On the other hand, *distance education* is a modality which permits the delivery of a group of didactic media without the necessity of regular class participation, where the individual is responsible for his own learning.[21]

These definitions notwithstanding, terms such as 'open-learning institution', 'open university' and 'distance-teaching institution' are used quite freely throughout this book. In these cases, the reference is to educational institutions which formally identify themselves in this way (eg Athabasca University, the Open University, the Indira Gandhi

National Open University) and does not necessarily imply that they are more open than some other institutions on any particular dimension.

'Open Management' is an approach to the management of such organizations which is modelled on the value systems on which they are based. This concept is discussed in more detail in Chapter 5.

Institutional barriers to openness

While open-learning institutions have been established to help students overcome such barriers to a further education as geographical distance, financial and time constraints, and restrictive admission policies, there are other less obvious barriers, some of which emanate from the institutions themselves.

It is one thing to adopt a policy of openness and quite another to carry it out successfully. It is ironic that some of the following are derived directly from attempts to institutionalize open learning:

Traditional staff. Given their relative newness, it is not surprising that open-learning institutions are staffed mainly from the ranks of traditional universities and colleges. While there are strong elements of self-selection, it is also frequently the case that academics apply for and accept positions in such institutions more because of job availability than dedication to the principles of open learning. Especially given the power of faculty in any university, such staff may dominate university governance, resulting in much more conservative institutions than was originally intended.

Traditional students. Harris writes persuasively about the 'hidden curriculum' which arises from resource limitations, from the unintended consequences of various assessment schemes and, most strongly, from the 'unstated but powerful and often highly conventional expectations of pupils or colleagues in practice'.[22] This suggests that our institutions have to educate their students not only in the formal curriculum but about open learning as well.

Invisible students. In many open learning situations, the student is seldom or never 'on campus'. While some academics sardonically refer to this as one of the great benefits of such institutions, in practice, it is a major problem. Staff who are not in daily contact with students can quickly lose their primary student orientation, so that registry clerks may be slower in responding to problems, faculty take longer to mark assignments, and tutors do not have the same commitment to an individual they would have in face-to-face situations. Senior administrators may be even further removed from the day-to-day problems faced by their students than they are at a campus-based institution. This invisibility may be particularly important in adult education where institutional staff need to be reminded from time to time that their students usually lead very busy lives, with several other identities (spouse, parent, career) often taking precedence over that of student (unlike the pattern for most full-time students aged between 18 and 22). Adult students may lack the skills to organize their competing priorities and may require assistance from the institution in ways which they may find difficult to articulate.

Never-ending academic year. In cases where students can enrol at the beginning of any month (as at Athabasca University), there is no formal beginning or end to the academic year. After a while, this can be very demoralizing for staff, for whom the work never ceases. In the traditional semester system, even if it has been a 'bad' year, at least it comes to an end; the lecturer can sigh, say 'Thank goodness, it's over', and enjoy a break before getting a fresh start in the new year.

Fiscal factors. Given that open-learning systems are often justified in terms of their cost efficiency and effectiveness, there may be a tendency to cut back on resources required for student support, so that a critical component of the commitment to open learning, support for the individual student, is compromised. For example, liberal extension and suspension policies which allow students to buy extra time for the completion of their courses may penalize other students waiting for a course place and may reduce success rates by tacitly encouraging procrastination. This is a sensible argument for reducing or eliminating them, but it may be at a cost to the openness and flexibility that is supposedly driving all decision-making.

While there is an implicit assumption throughout this book that 'open' is usually better than 'closed', it does not necessarily follow that a specific educational provision is always better the more open it is. It has already been noted that a completely open programme would not require an institution at all, and virtually every so-called open institution has elements that are quite closed.

For example, a specific training programme for the employees of a given company is obviously closed in its admissions, and yet may be very open in every other way. Other projects might have open admissions but quite rigid requirements as to when the students attend classes or take centralized examinations.

As Lewis[23] and others have demonstrated, one can establish an ideal-type against which existing institutions can be measured to determine their degrees of openness. While it may be an interesting intellectual exercise to compare various institutions in terms of their degree of openness, debates over which institutions are more open than others are trivial at best.

In each case, the ultimate test should be that the rationale for a given provision or requirement is seen as being in the best interests of the particular student group for whom it is intended. There will, of course, always be great debate about this – many institutional arrangements supposedly for the students' 'own good' have a lot more to do with convenience to their staff or to fiscal concerns. It is all too easy to dismiss these, but there will always be practical and resource-based limitations on openness and flexibility.

Furthermore, some restrictions and limitations can be justified as being in the students' own interests. For example, it is usually reasonable to require students to take a prerequisite course before admitting them to a course which they otherwise have almost no hope of passing. Subject matter which requires social interaction may not be conducive to home study or may require educational media which are not necessarily accessible to everyone.

The ideal-type presented above for open learning, combined with the notion of 'value-driven leadership' (see Chapter 5), offers a useful model for the management of open learning. The values are derived from the ideal type, and it is up to each institution to be very clear on where it stands on each (for example, open admissions, degree of flexibility in learning systems, control of content). Once defined, these values can then be set out as criteria for planning and decision-making in the organization.

It is argued below that if our institutions are to be as open as we say they are (and it does not take very much insight to recognize that they are not), management too must be open and driven by the same values which are represented in the organization's mission statements and strategic plans. This argument is developed further in the next two chapters and then tested against selected practical examples in Part 3.

Notes

1. Illich, I D (1971), *Deschooling Society,* London: Calder & Boyars.
2. Fletcher, B (1968), *Universities in the Modern World,*London: Pergamon Press.
3. Ibid, p 14.
4. Ibid, pp 15–17.
5. Butts, R F (1955), *A Cultural History of Western Education: Its Social and Intellectual Foundations,* New York: McGraw-Hill.

6. Ibid, chapters 3–5, pp 19–44.
7. Ibid, p 24.
8. Ibid, p 38.
9. Rumble, G (1989), '"Open Learning", "Distance Learning", and the Misuse of Language' in *Open Learning* (June), pp 32–40.
10. Lewis, R (1990), 'Open Learning and the Misuse of Language: A Response to Greville Rumble', *Open Learning*, 4(3), February.
11. Illich, op cit.
12. See, for example, MacIntosh, N and Morrison, V (1968), 'Student Demand, Progress and Withdrawal: The Open University's First Four Years', *Higher Education Review*, 7, pp 37–66; Woodley, A (1986), 'Distance Students in the United Kingdom', *Open Learning* (June), pp 11–13; and Woolfe, R (1974), 'Social Equality as an Open University Objective', *Teaching at a Distance,* 1, pp 41–44.
13. Harris, D (1988), 'The Micro-Politics of Openness', *Open Learning*, 3(2), June, p 14.
14. See, for example, Thompson, G. (1989), 'Provision of Student Support Services in Distance Education: Do We Know What They Need?' in Sweet, R (ed), *Post-Secondary Distance Education in Canada,* Athabasca: Athabasca University and CSSE, pp 43–50; and Inglis, P (1985), 'Promoting Positive Learning Attitudes Through Personalizing External Studies: A Study of the Learning Experiences of 50 Weipa (Far North Queensland) Students', Paper presented at Melbourne ICDE Conference, no 1039.
15. Morrison, T R (1989), 'Beyond Legitimacy: Facing the Future in Distance Education' in *International Journal of Lifelong Education,* 8, 1 (Jan–Mar), p 9.
16. Lewis, R, op cit; and Lewis, R (1986), 'What is Open Learning?', *Open Learning,* 1(2), pp 5–10.
17. Rumble, op cit, p 33.
18. See, for example, Paine, N (ed) (1988), *Open Learning in Transition: An Agenda for Action,* Cambridge: National Extension College; and Thorpe, M and Grugeon, D (1987), *Open Learning for Adults,* London: Longman.
19. Rumble, op cit, p 37.
20. Ibid, p 34.
21. Escotet, M (1980), 'Adverse Factors in the Development of an Open University in Latin America', *Programme Learning and Educational Technology,* 17 (4), p 144.
22. Harris, op cit, p 14.
23. Lewis, op cit.

CHAPTER 4

Academic Autonomy and
Open-Learning Systems

Chapter synopsis

A practical exploration of the challenges and dilemmas faced by academics working in open universities highlights some of the inherent conflicts between traditional and nontraditional values in open learning. The chapter offers a number of suggestions as to how these problems can be overcome in orientating and leading academic staff in open universities.

Traditional and modern approaches

A recent article in *The Globe and Mail* newspaper[1] discussed the dilemmas faced by university search committees seeking a president in today's society. The range of expectations for such positions is so great and demanding that its author concluded that 'the only possible winner would have to be divine'.[2]

While, traditionally, universities were usually satisfied to recruit men (gender deliberate) of strong moral character with a solid academic record and an effective public presence, today's criteria are rather more extensive. Generic skills such as strategic planning, marketing and fund-raising are so much a part of the requisite repertoire for a university president that 'head-hunters' are increasingly looking outside the academic community for such leaders. The argument is that the very much increased involvement of governments and taxpayers in university funding and governance brings universities more into the mainstream of society and hence requires the same sorts of leadership skills demonstrated by those most effective in the corporate sector.

Some university presidents, such as Carleton University's Robin Farquhar,[3] strongly oppose such trends, claiming that an intimate knowledge of how universities function is essential to success in the presidential role, a viewpoint similar to that attributed to Millet in Chapter 3. This perspective asserts that the long traditions of collegiality and faculty autonomy, essential planks in preserving academic freedom and the pursuit of the truth outside political interference, require an experience and sensitivity which can only be gained by participation in such institutions. The argument usually is that what are perceived to be the more autocratic and 'top-down' methods of the private sector are incompatible with the authority basis of the 'community of scholars'.

This perspective is often advanced by academics as an argument against the presence of management at all (notably in Britain where, at least, at the Open University, an underlying suspicion of 'management' in a university persists even among many supervisors). Ironically, while some university academics continue to resist any challenge to the *collegium*, more and more businesses are emulating aspects of collegial models of governance and decision-making as they cope with the challenges of managing highly specialized professionals. Charles Handy argues quite persuasively that, in a knowledge society, with its emphasis on information, intelligence and ideas, where a business's search for quality can be equated to a university's search for truth, corporations will increasingly come to resemble universities or colleges.[4] The corollary is that universities are also going to look more and more like businesses.

Without denying the importance of engaging executive officers who are experienced in and sensitive to collegial modes of governance, the position taken here is that today's university leaders must be far more than collegially orientated decision-makers. Demands for public accountability, the range and complexity of goals and expectations for universities, the challenges of collective bargaining, and the need to raise resources beyond those supplied directly by government all require university leaders who are both skilled managers and effective academics.

As has already been suggested, there are strong conflicts between the academic's quest for freedom and autonomy and the bureaucratic demands of systems in complex organizations. Nowhere is this more evident than in an open university employing traditional university academics.[5]

In a conventional university, a faculty member is hired primarily for his or her research and carries a teaching load which, once sanctioned by the department in terms of content and timetable, is largely left to the practitioner to 'get on with' in the classroom. Even where there are student evaluations of faculty members, an academic's teaching competence and style are seldom influenced much or dealt with by the larger organization.

Contrast this with the role of faculty member at an open-learning institution. For example, an academic arriving at Athabasca University will find:*

A. No students on campus. While this may sometimes be cited as a positive by the more cynical, it is one of the biggest disadvantages of distance education. The student advocacy role tends to be undermined as academic staff are further removed from their primary clientele, it is harder to promote and support research without the aid and incentive of graduate students, and the vibrancy of a traditional campus is sorely missed by many.

B. Course teams. Courses are developed by course teams where the faculty member may be joined by other subject-matter experts, instructional designers, editors and visual designers; hence, the faculty member shares accountability with these staff in a manner foreign to most on-campus teachers.

C. Critical path deadlines. While having to meet regular classes imposes deadlines on the campus-based faculty member, he or she has at least some control over what happens in each class. In distance education, the academic is required to meet a series of strict deadlines for the production of a course, failing which it may not appear at all during the semester for which it was originally intended.

D. An integrated production process. This means that the services of the media-production department or course-materials inventory are as important for the delivery of the course as the faculty member's own preparation. This tends to break down traditional distinctions between the 'academic' and 'support' or 'service' divisions of the institution, and it requires a kind of matrix management which cuts across such distinctions between 'academic' and 'administrative' executive officers, who are unusually sensitive to the requirements of their 'opposite' divisions.

E. Printed course packages. The printed finished product is not delivered behind closed doors in a classroom but is available for all, students and professional colleagues alike, to scrutinize and evaluate.

F. Off-campus tutors. Although the academic retains overall responsibility for a course, it is usually an off-campus tutor who has direct

*Please note that the following is an abridged version of my article 'Staff Development Needs for Universities: Mainstream and Distance Education', which appears in Smith and Kelly (1987), Chapter 8.

contact with the students and whom the latter regard as the 'teacher'. This requires the academic to be more of an administrator and course coordinator, roles in which he or she may have had little prior experience or predilection. One of the most common problems facing new faculty members at Athabasca University is the amount of administration which tutor monitoring and supervision requires.

G. A never-ending academic year. There is no obvious beginning or end to the academic year – new students enrol at the beginning of each month, and there are no 'slack' periods when few students require attention. Academics used to the rhythms of semester systems and to extended periods for research usually find this quite an adjustment, both in terms of managing their various tasks and in coping psychologically with the absence of a clear beginning and end to the year. Even though there are no classes to meet, the faculty member will have to call upon unusual time-management skills in such a system to avoid strong perceptions of too much administration and too little time for research.

H. Lack of stimulation. With no students on campus and colleagues working somewhat independently on their own course preparations, there is not the same academic atmosphere or concept of 'campus' that provides basic socialization and stimulation to academics in a mainstream institution. Indeed, as microprocessing and computer networks increasingly facilitate the ability of a faculty member to work at home, traditional modes of supervision are less and less appropriate. Charles Handy has cited this as a keystone of future organizations, and the experience of those involved in distance education is again relevant for the management of many different sorts of organizations.[6] The implications of this trend for such cornerstones of good management as strong human-relations skills and management by walking around are quite astounding and suggest the need for quite dramatically new ways of leading, coordinating and motivating others by 'managing at a distance'.

I. Traditional vs nontraditional staff. Many institutions like Athabasca University, deliberately set up to be 'different', have attracted nontraditional staff who may be quite opposed to the values of mainstream academics. Hence, the latter may be quite surprised to find colleagues who do not accept the importance they ascribe to such concepts as disciplinary research, graduate work or improving the university's reputation among mainstream universities. A healthy tension between these perspectives can be very stimulating and productive, but outright conflict can be debilitating for an institution if these different perspectives are not resolved over a period of time.[7]

The question of credibility

Over and above all these tangible and readily identifiable differences is a more subtle one – the insecurity that comes with being part of a relatively new field of endeavour. Especially because its roots are in correspondence education, which many people still associate with drawing courses advertised on the back pages of comic books, distance education does not yet enjoy the status of more traditional modes of scholarship. One can be forgiven for suspecting that this is in Lewis's mind when he deplores the 'confusion of "open learning" with "distance learning" or (even worse) with "correspondence courses"'.[8]

There are tremendous ironies in this. Open-learning institutions may bend over backwards to recruit established academics from conventional universities to enhance their own academic reputations, even when those academics may not be as well suited to the tasks at hand as someone from a less conventional background. Experience has shown that university academics, especially if unchecked by editors and instructional designers, have a tendency to overload courses prepared for home study, primarily because they know that, unlike their classroom teaching, which is hardly ever observed by peers, their 'open' courses will be in the public domain and available for scrutiny by other academics. As a consequence, their first concern is that these courses be unquestionably respectable academically.

A fascinating depiction of this process is contained in a chapter by Bruce King in the recent book edited by Terry Evans and Daryl Nation, *Critical Reflections on Distance Education*.[9] Describing the agonies endured by a course team in preparing a programme-development module for a Diploma in Distance Education, King admits that the course team was two-thirds of the way through the process when they recognized that their preoccupation with academic credibility had led them to abandon their commitment to respect and build on the skills and perspectives of their student practitioners.

> A major cause of our difficulties was the sense that for the course to be academically respectable the team had to get it 'right'. Recognition that this degree of staff determination for what counted for knowledge and how it was to be accessed was 'getting it wrong' was liberating both for our students and for the team.[10]

Before my perspective is misinterpreted, I should note that I have long been a strong advocate of engaging full-time academic faculty with commitments to research and scholarship in their respective fields to open-learning institutions. This model, represented by Athabasca University and Britain's Open University, contrasts with and is more expensive than that employed at other institutions, such as the Open University of British Columbia, where courses are written almost exclusively by external academics. The inclusion of full-time in-house faculty also introduces more traditional notions of academic freedom and autonomy, as well as collegial modes of governance whereby departmental councils and elected senates have considerable decision- and policy-making authority. This complicates decision-making and can lead to situations in which concerns of academic autonomy and control conflict directly with systems requirements or the perceived needs of students.

As an advocate of this model despite its expense, in terms both financial and administrative, I believe that maintaining high academic standards is essential to the success of an open-learning institution and that traditional norms of academic freedom and commitment to research are an integral part of this quest. If a university is going to offer programmes and courses in a disciplinary area, it is important that its staff include fully qualified in-house academics who can ensure the integrity and credibility of these offerings.

The hiring of external academics to write specific courses is part of this quest for quality, in that it gives a relatively small institution access to the best available experts in any given field, but it is also important for the institution to retain control over this development. I reached this conclusion not long after arriving at Athabasca University in 1980, when there were a lot of problems with an economics course written by an external academic when there was no one in-house fully competent to assess the academic merits of what had been produced.

There are many different possible responses to the dilemmas posed above for new faculty coming for the first time to an open university. Some adapt much more readily than others and find ways to preserve what is important to them in their new environment. Some, especially those who are fairly independent in their working habits, prefer the freedom offered by an institution with no formal classes. Others find the relative lack of institutionally imposed rhythms very difficult to handle, and they become frustrated by their own misuse of time or miss the socialization more readily offered by campus-based institutions.

The differences in the atmosphere and expectations for university academics raise interesting questions in considering such traditional concerns as tenure and promotions. Does 'success' at a traditional university guarantee similar results in an open university? Should someone with a tenure at a campus-based institution receive a tenure appointment at an open university? Particularly as a result of similar emphases on research and scholarship, there is probably a strong correlation between performances in both institutions, but there are clearly differences which discriminate among abilities and which should be carefully scrutinized in hiring and tenure decisions in an open university.

A development prototype

Athabasca University has a very traditional set of terms and conditions for its academic staff. Promotion is based primarily on research and publication, with success in course development as the other major factor. This has not always been the case. In fact, some of the earliest academics were hired by Athabasca with the expressed understanding that they were expected to focus on course development and delivery, and to devote little time to their own disciplinary research. In at least one case, this has proved awkward subsequently when someone hired with this expectation was then denied promotion because he had not published enough! There are enough similar stories from other open universities, such as those in the United Kingdom and The Netherlands, to suggest that most open universities are on the same evolutionary path and that one could develop a prototype for their development. Without taking this too seriously, it might begin to look something like the following (perhaps the International Council for Distance Education (ICDE) should fund a formal effort to develop this model and hence save all those new institutions countless hours of replicating the practices and mistakes of their predecessors):

The first few years will focus on course development with large and comprehensive course teams. It will soon be realized that the teams are too large and diverse to get the work done on time and soon students will be complaining that courses aren't ready when promised. It will be discovered that smaller, more pragmatically established teams get the work done more quickly, and courses will be produced at an accelerated rate.

Once a core component of courses is developed, someone will publish discouraging figures about very low completion rates, and attention will shift to better student support and tutorial services, and more resources will be put into regional networks. This will help marginally, but there will be debates about the costs of course development and delivery vis-à-vis student success. Someone will propose that it makes a lot of sense to develop courses collaboratively with another institution, but this will never work as well as intended. Then, concerns about the academic reputation of the institution will lead to increased pressures for research and publication. Another pressure for this will be that the university is not quite sure what to do with all the full-time permanent faculty it originally hired, now that the demand for new courses has slowed down.

One response to this will be to encourage faculty to go back and revise courses which are increasingly out-of-date, but this will be very difficult because hardly anyone likes doing revisions. As a result, there will be pressure for new programmes so that new courses can be developed and new markets generated. Because such responses satisfy both faculty and administrative interests (keeping enrolments up, being seen to do 'new' things), the institution will embark on yet another cycle of development and expansion, including a significant investment in international projects which will take far more time, resources and overhead than had ever been anticipated and will end up being completely different from the project originally anticipated, but will nevertheless be a great learning experience for all involved.

The expansionist mode will continue until, after several years of budget slashing, the institution threatens to 'implode' from strains on its infrastructure, leading to a complete requestioning of its ambitions and, very frequently, to new leadership at the top. If the institution is fortunate, it will attract leaders who will continue to challenge it to develop and expand while finding new and better ways to carry out its functions more cost-effectively or changing its functions altogether. Otherwise, the institution will lose a lot of innovation and dynamism as it undergoes a period of consolidation and conservatism.

Every time I discuss these sorts of developments with those in other institutions, there is mutual recognition that we are all on the same paths, experiencing similar pressures and responding similarly. The rub comes from the equally common recognition that, even though we agree that we all do the same sorts of things, every one of us insists on going through the process our own way anyhow. 'Why should I learn from you when I can learn so much more effectively from my own mistakes?' is the apparent message.

While it is dangerous to generalize about effectiveness in as personal and complex a world as academia, it follows that the particular demands of open universities (off-campus delivery of courses, more administrative duties, less direct contact with fellow academics and students, unfamiliar academic year) are better suited to faculty who are more independent and have better time-management and administrative skills. Faculty who need the constant stimulation of students and colleagues, and/or those who respond best to such extrinsic motivators as being prepared for each class may find the atmosphere in an open university less conducive to their style of working. It does not take much insight to see that it is the same sort of characteristic required of students in open-learning institutions that defines effective staff members, such as an ability to work independently and to manage one's own time.

While the above tendencies suggest some guidelines for hiring academics at open universities, they should not be used to absolve the institution of responsibility for assisting its new staff to cope with the unique demands of working in open learning. Indeed, universities thrive on diversity, and staff not as naturally suited to the open environment may nevertheless bring vital skills and orientations to their positions (eg research, disciplinary expertise, strong writing skills).

The onus should thus be on the institution to conduct a thorough recruiting process which emphasizes the differences confronting academic staff used to campus-based positions. This is easier said than done, for academics recruited from this sector will usually want reassurance that the institution is a 'good' university* and that it will provide as much support for their research and other scholarly activities as their present institution does. It is misleading, however, to suggest that the differences are trivial, and a lot of subsequent grief will be avoided if the newcomer is fully aware of the challenges that he or she will face, including the already listed absence of students on campus, course-team approach to course development, additional administrative and supervisory loads, and different rhythms of the academic year.

This need not be a negative exercise, for many of the differences can be cited as advantages. Without the disruption of regular classes to meet, a well-organized faculty member has more, not less, control over his or her time and can organize it best to suit his or her particular working style. The institution can also encourage faculty to do some tutoring or classroom teaching to ensure that its academics don't get too far removed from their students.

Moreover, many open-university staff whose primary previous teaching experience has been with young undergraduates in large universities will be pleasantly surprised by the calibre and commitment of adult students and the incredible motivation they display in taking advantage of the opportunity to pursue a university education in their own time and place.

A sensitive and individually focused orientation programme run by academic colleagues is probably the most effective way to introduce new staff. Without being overly prescriptive, the approach advocated here is one which views new staff members from the same perspective as the institution sees its new students. They bring a lot to the institution but will have to face some very unusual challenges which require considerable independence and skills but which also require strong personal support from those who have been through it all before.

The following would be useful components of such an orientation programme,[11] although resistance to anything too formally labelled

---

*Although perceptions are changing, it is doubtless more often than not the case that 'good' is defined as being most like a traditional university prototype, such as Oxbridge or Harvard.

'staff development' should never be underestimated, and most of these components may, in fact, be best achieved in much less formal ways than are suggested here:

- An introduction to the mission, history and philosophy of the institution, with reference to other open- and distance-learning institutions;
- Seminars and other interactive sessions focusing on the students – who they are, what they are looking for, factors in their success and failure in this mode of learning (supported by well-documented data from institutional researchers);
- Discussions about the implications of the second point above for course design and delivery;
- Special sessions on instructional design led by professional staff trained in this area (instructional developers, editors, experienced faculty course-writers);
- Feedback and strategy sessions on various ways of tutoring (by telephone, correspondence, computer, etc);
- Informal sessions with colleagues which emphasize the unique challenges of working in such an environment (no students on campus, different rhythm to the work week, staff working independently and in isolation from each other, managing off-campus tutors, etc);
- Opportunities to meet face-to-face with students to understand better the challenges they face and the services and support which have enabled them to succeed.

In the longer run, these initial orientation seminars should be complemented by a regular staff-development programme which includes, in addition to research and scholarship seminars:

- Time-management seminars;
- Travel, professional development, and research funds to encourage academics to visit other open-learning institutions and to develop their expertise in coping with their own institution's particular demands;
- Periodic presentations of institutional research on the factors which have an impact on student success, such as the effectiveness of information and counselling services, different approaches to tutoring and course design, and the application of new technologies.

While it is a large order to recruit top academics who share the institution's strong commitments to open admissions, open learning and lifelong learning, it is getting easier as the success of such institutions as Britain's Open University becomes known, and the increasing interest in distance education and open learning on conventional university campuses spreads. The challenges are great, but if the commitment to open management is as strong as the belief in open learning, the result will be an institution which provides strong leadership in the extension of access to and success in high-quality university education to a broader cross-section of the general populace.

Notes

1. French, O (1989), 'Universities Aim for Big Catch in Small Presidential Pool', *The Globe and Mail,* 10 July, pp A1, A9.
2. Ibid, p A1.
3. Ibid.
4. Handy, C (1989), *The Age of Unreason,* London: Business Books, p 113.
5. It would be wrong to carry the contrasts too far, however, for campus-based universities themselves are changing quite dramatically. Ever increasing enrolments, combined with sustained cuts in budgets have increased pressures for accountability, and the typical university is nowhere near the ivory tower it was as recently as 1960.
6. Handy, op cit, pp 84–7.
7. For an analysis of this issue, see Paul, R H (1985), 'Traditional and Non-Traditional Values: The Politics of Distance Education', *Proceedings of the Thirteenth World Conference,* ICDE, Melbourne, August, no 1171; and Abrioux, D, Paul, R, Shale, D, and Thomas, D (1984), 'Non-Traditional Education and Organizational Change: The Case of Athabasca University', paper presented at the AERA/ASHE Conference, San Francisco, 28 October.
8. Lewis, R (1988), 'The Open Schools?' in Nigel Paine (ed), *Open Learning in Transition: An Agenda for Action,* Cambridge: National Extension College, p 257.
9. King, B (1989), 'Teaching Distance Education' in Evans, T and Nation, D (eds), *Critical Reflections on Distance Education,* London: Falmer Press, pp 95–122.
10. Ibid, p 121.
11. For a fuller discussion, see Paul, R H (1987), 'Staff Development Needs for Universities: Mainstream and Distance Education' in Smith, P and Kelly, M (eds), *Distance Education and the Mainstream,* London: Croom Helm, pp 150–1.

CHAPTER 5

Towards Open Management:
A Value-Driven Leadership Approach

Chapter synopsis

Building on the organizational models for higher education presented in Chapter 2, this chapter adovates the concept of open management, leadership based on the value-driven approach advocated by Badaracco and Ellsworth.

The brief review in Chapter 2 of organizational models for universities demonstrated that, while each has much to contribute to the understanding, management and leadership of universities, none is sufficient in itself. In fact, the overwhelming conclusion is that universities are complex organizations which can be better understood with reference to all four models examined above.

Their basic structures are bureaucratic, and many of the operating procedures of traditional bureaucracies are essential to their continuing operation. They are organized into faculties where decision-making retains many of the hallmarks of collegiality, but it would be both naive and misleading to ignore the importance of interest groups, collective bargaining and conflict theory in interpreting planning, policy development and decision-making on campus. Any suggestion that these three models (bureaucratic, collegial, political) can be combined into a neat, legal-rational explanation of university governance and management is countered by Cohen and March's emphasis on ambiguity, fluidity and change, and on the concept of a university as an 'organized anarchy'.[1] The answer, then, is not in yet another organizational model, but in the concept of leadership.

The importance of institutional leadership

Today's challenges place a very high premium on institutional leadership, that which develops a clear and coherent sense of direction and a comprehensive and value-driven way of getting there. It represents the practical application of what has been learned about leading people in other settings, notably the corporate world, informed by what the various models of universities as organizations tell us about the particular requirements of that milieu. It is leadership that can encompass a number of management and governance styles; a sense of purpose and direction that will provide meaning for and integration of the various activities and functions throughout the institution.

My own notion of excellence suggests that an effective university will have:

(1) A clear statement of purpose and direction and long-range and strategic plans to outline how these will be achieved.
(2) A strong and collegial faculty with the academic freedom to pursue excellence in their given fields.
(3) Good bureaucratic systems which ensure the effective functioning of the entire support structure for students and faculty alike.
(4) Strong leadership to bring these component parts together and to give integrity to the institution.
(5) Leaders with the wisdom, perspective and sense of humour to function effectively in the setting of organized anarchy.

Point 4 is a pivotal one for purposes of this book. All good universities must be strong in areas 1 to 3 above, but it is leadership that will ultimately make the difference between good and excellent institutions. Leadership, rather than management, is the integrating force that brings the requisite components together and gives direction and meaning in the context of the institution's *raison d'être*.

While much attention is paid here to the various techniques of administration and management, leadership, which is vital to the success of any organization, involves a lot more than just technique. Bennis and Nanus state that too many organizations are 'overmanaged and underled'.[2] The role of senior executives is to provide leadership – which encourages people to manage themselves.

It does not necessarily follow, however, that the effective university leader is one who simply applies bureaucratic, collegial or political styles of decision-making on the appropriate occasion. Some writers have imagined the leader as a sort of superhuman figure with a plethora of styles and responses in his or her arsenal. Following an incisive analysis of just which response is required for the occasion at hand, the leader provides the appropriate style (political, *laissez-faire*, directive, collegial). This is a slightly caricatured representation of the 'situational leadership'[3] style of decision-making which has been in vogue until recently.

Value-driven leadership

The preferred approach suggested here is closer to that advocated by
Badaracco and Ellsworth in their stimulating book *Leadership and the
Quest for Integrity*[4], which is a treatise against the notion of situational
leadership. Instead, like Bennis and Nanus, they stress the importance
of 'integrity' in leadership, a consistent philosophy which governs how
the individual acts in all aspects of his or her leadership role. They argue
that very few individuals, if any, have either the foresight to know which
style to apply in each case or the acting ability to carry out each style with
equal effectiveness. There are significant dangers that leaders will adopt
what is subsequently found to be inappropriate responses or that their
credibility will be undermined by the hypocrisy of trying to be what they
are not.

Like Cohen and March, Badaracco and Ellsworth start with the
ambiguity of organizations, which are, in reality, far from the ideal and
clear sorts of institutions suggested by theory. Theirs is a leadership
model, one which argues for 'prejudice', a preconceived bias to
handling things in a certain integrated way.[5] They go on to describe
three basic leadership philosophies – political, directive and value-
driven – and present the best case for each in applying them to day-to-
day issues. Each approach is described in terms of its fundamental
assumptions about people and organizations.[6]

The *political leader* views people as being motivated primarily by self-
interest and a search for power, wealth and coherence in the face of the
self-interest of others. He or she moves forward in small, incremental
steps, orchestrating everything astutely from behind the scenes. Other
characteristics are flexibility, adaptability and extreme pragmatism in
all decision making.

The *directive leader* finds this view of mankind too limited for explaining people's motivations, and places more emphasis on an individual's
competitive nature and quest for self-actualization. A hands-on, open
individual with a high tolerance for conflict and a very clearly focused
view of where the organization should be going, he or she sets very high
standards and does everything possible to drive everyone to meet them.

The *value-driven leader* believes that creating something of value is
the ultimate expression of one's individuality, that people need to find
meaning in life through their work. He or she is dedicated to the task of
'energizing followers to take actions that support higher corporate
purposes and not their own self-interests'.[7] The essence of this
philosophy is to lead by example.

A leader must be an exemplar to the organization, demanding the highest standards of integrity, and be doggedly consistent in word and deed in all matters affecting the company's values.[8]

This is not to suggest that such a leader will not be political, pragmatic and directive, but it is important to note that, when the chips are down, he or she will never compromise on values fundamental to his or her philosophy or to the mission and goals of the organization.

After applying each of the philosophies to five basic 'dilemmas' common to all organizations, Badaracco and Ellsworth conclude that an appropriate combination of directive and value-driven leadership is the most effective approach. While the political approach is extremely useful on occasion, it is dangerous in the long run as its essential pragmatism can undermine institutional values.

There are some problems with the Badaracco and Ellsworth book. After a fairly clear presentation of the 'political', 'directive' and 'value-driven' approaches, one would expect them to opt for one of these or to suggest that an individual decide which of the three best suited his or her style and hence to adopt that one systematically and consistently forever after. Their recognition that none of their three philosophies is sufficient in itself and their consequent advocacy of a 'melding' of the directive and value-driven approaches can be seen to undermine the strength of their assertions in favour of a clear bias and against situational leadership. Given this 'hedge', one wonders whether their approach is really very different from the 'chameleon' view of leadership they so decry.[9] In fact, it would be fairly easy to rewrite their basic premises as supportive of rather than opposed to situational leadership. Moreover, one could postulate more philosophies than the three they explore, such as a '*laissez-faire*' or '*humanistic*' approach.

However valid these concerns, they do not negate their basic premise – that a philosophy of management driven by strong inner values which are consistent with the overall goals of the institution is fundamental to successful leadership. Bennis and Nanus also stress that integrity (consistency and constancy in approaches to decision-making) is fundamental to the development of 'trust', the 'lubrication that makes it possible for organizations to work.'[10]

In a videotaped interview for an Athabasca University programme in leadership development for school admnistrators, former University of Alberta president Myer Horowitz, a giant among Canadian university administrators, emphasized the importance of integrity in management. While counselling patience and a long-term view which respected the importance of helping people to adjust to change and to deal with it, he made it abundantly clear that no attention to political agenda or expediency should ever be at the expense of a leader's fundamental values.[11]

This is the approach on which this book is based and which will be applied to the many practical examples which follow. That is, while all leaders and managers must be judged on their results, the way they achieve something is always at least as important as what they achieve, for it will ultimately pattern the values and behaviour of those around them. Only through a value-driven approach can a leader achieve real change, change which is open, which is permanent, and which inspires all involved to understand it and to make it effective.

While the central argument is for a value-driven approach, this is not to suggest that basic values need constantly to be articulated. In fact, the effectiveness of leaders like Dr Horowitz is that their strongest values are underlying ones which only become evident with time. A manager who resorts too frequently to statements of very basic values will face far more conflict and opposition, as those in disagreement will feel compelled to defend their own basic value system where it is different. While the institutional value system should be well articulated and understood from the outset, the leader's strongest values should become evident more from long-term example than constant reiteration of them. In short, a strong leader may be highly flexible or quite directive, but his or her underlying value system will almost never be compromised.

Value-driven leadership is not easily achieved, for it sometimes requires the leader to buck current trends, to take positions which are longer-term in focus and may be unpopular in the short term. One of the concerns about modern democratic forms of government, driven as they are to winning elections every four years or so, is that they force a short-term perspective on the party in power, a perspective which makes it extremely difficult to deal with basic, long-term issues, such as the elimination of the national debt.

In writing this section, I am conscious of the occasions when I have gone along with decisions with which I was quite uncomfortable because they were contrary to my basic values, and of other times when I fought hard for those values long after it was clear that I had 'lost' the issue. I still regret the former and recognize that my reiteration of my own values after a contrary decision was made by my superior was usually a negative factor in the organization. This is not to suggest that one must abandon values if they are not prevailing, but to recognize the importance of promoting them positively in the organization rather than refighting battles that have already been lost.

The various models of higher education outlined in Chapter 2 have contributed a great deal to our understanding of the management and governance of colleges and universities, but none is, in itself, completely satisfactory. However, each contributes an important piece to the puzzle

– the bureaucratic structures, the collegial mode of decision-making, the politics of university governance, and the organized chaos of the whole organization. Rather than offer yet another organizational model here, a value-driven leadership approach has been advocated. Under such an approach, the top management team of an institution or business, defines and articulates a clear set of guiding values and principles which form the basis for decision-making. However much is subsequently delegated and however decentralized the distribution of power and authority, it is always the chief executive officer's primary responsibility to ensure that these central values drive all decision-making in the organization.

The better articulated and the more universally accepted these central values, the more collegial the decision-making. Where there is dispute over, resistance to, or apathy about some of these values, senior management will have to resort to more political measures or, on occasion, to the exertion of its line authority down the bureaucracy.

The real skill of management is knowing when – and when not – to intervene. Typically, too little effort goes into the 'front-end' process of defining and articulating the institution's values and mission, and too much goes into intervening when things don't work out. What is advocated here is an approach which puts far more emphasis on the front-end, so that senior administrators become tireless crusaders for the central institutional values. In the author's opinion, there is no single criterion more important to the success of a university president (or any corporate chief-executive officer) than the ability to communicate effectively and persuasively his or her commitment to a fundamental set of mutually consistent values which drive all decision-making in the institution.

Of course, zeal is a double-edged sword, and it must be tempered by sensitivity to those receiving the message (rather than, we hope, the sword thrust!). The whole community should be involved in developing and subsequently refining the institutional mission and values so that there is strong and thorough ownership of them. It is a community process, but it also involves 'having out' some fundamental issues. This is where the collegiality can break down and the process become more political.

It is in the face of conflict and the inevitable chaos of a complex institution like a university that the real effectiveness of a leader is tested. A strong sense of purpose and direction is critical, but it must be assisted by sensitivity to those affected by decisions, by good political judgment (notably in being able to identify the major issues where intervention is essential and the less important ones which can be left to internal processes), and, perhaps above all else, by a good sense of humour.

Open management may not be the easiest way to lead an organization, especially because it exposes the leader more often than do more bureaucratic and hierarchical systems. It may also be more time-consuming, in that there may be more debates about the values underlying decisions, and in its tendency to encourage challenges and dissent. On the other hand, the leader who takes time to develop and articulate clearly his or her own approach to management and to education will have a set of principles to guide most decision-making, and this may save time in the long run.

Of course, open management means different things to different people and in different contexts, especially given that 'open' is a relative term (as already seen in our discussion of open learning). My own definition follows naturally from the details of my personal philosophy of education and management which were set out in Chapter 1 (pp 22–3, above).

Summary: the concept of open management

For purposes of this book, open management has the following characteristics:

- It is driven by the basic values which are central to the mission and integrity of the organization and its mandate;
- Its practitioners are dedicated to defining, articulating and implementing the central mandate of an institution but are open and flexible in the ways that it is achieved;
- It is carried out in an organizational climate in which managers are directly accountable both for their decisions and for the way they go about making them, and in which power and authority are achieved as much as they are ascribed;
- While many different styles of management can be incorporated within an open management system, none should be opposed to the basic values of the institution and its leaders.

It is one thing to develop a coherent philosophy of open learning and quite another to implement it successfully. There is considerable difference between a philosophy of open management and its actual practice on a day-to-day basis. In Part 3, below, a number of typical practical dilemmas faced by the manager of distance- and open-learning systems are confronted, with particular emphasis on the usefulness of the value-driven leadership model. The model will be evaluated at the end of this section on the basis of its usefulness in resolving the standard dilemmas faced by open-learning systems managers.

Notes

1. Cohen, M D and March, J G (1974), *Leadership and Ambiguity,* New York: McGraw-Hill.
2. Bennis, W and Nanus, B (1985), *Leaders: The Strategies for Taking Charge,* New York: Harper & Row, p 21.
3. See, for example, Blanchard, K et al (1985), *Leadership and the One-Minute Manager: Increasing Effectiveness Through Situational Leadership,* New York: William Morrow & Co.
4. Badaracco, J L, Jr, and Ellsworth, R R (1989), *Leadership and the Quest for Integrity,* Boston: Harvard School of Business.
5. Ibid, p 4.
6. These are presented in Ibid, p 95.
7. Ibid, p 66.
8. Ibid, p 74.
9. Ibid, p 199.
10. Bennis and Nanus, op cit, p 43.
11. Paul, R H, 'Interview with Myer Horowitz', Videotape for Athabasca University's Leadership Development for School Administrators programme, University of Alberta, 1988.

Part 3: The Management of Open Learning: Practical Concerns

It is always debatable how important theory is to practice, and how much it has to do with the development of good managers. As with teaching, there are some who can step into a management position and do a superb job without prior experience, and there are others with strong theoretical backgrounds or all the experience in the world who are no better managers than they were in their first supervisory position.

In my own view, a theoretical perspective is essential to understanding and interpreting what goes on in practice and to helping a manager improve his or her performance. While there is no substitute for experience, it is useful only if the individual learns from it, can articulate it, and can recognize the factors that contributed to its successes and failures.

Part 3 focuses on the daily challenges of managing open learning. The true test of leadership and management ability comes on the firing line where people frequently have to make decisions and establish priorities in inadequate time frames and with less than sufficient information. Performance under fire also reveals a person's true values, not necessarily the ones he or she espouses on less stressful occasions.

Wherever applicable, case studies and examples from actual practice are used to illustrate the dilemmas, conflicts and challenges which every manager faces. Often the context is particular to my own experiences at Athabasca University, but it is the kind of issue rather than its specific details which is of critical importance.

The five chapters in this part explore in some detail four central challenges of open university management – finding appropriate ways to establish, respond to and evaluate the central concept of student success in such institutions; the particular problems of managing at a distance in the contexts of regional networks and off-campus tutors; planning and managing the integration of new technologies into teaching and administration; and collaborating with outside agencies in the achievement of one's own priorities.

Part 3: The Management of Apex Locating Pressure Conveyance

CHAPTER 6

Managing for Success: Learner Interaction and Independence

Chapter synopsis

The chapter focuses on the challenges students face in open-learning situations and on how their success can be measured. After an analysis of such traditional criteria as persistence and completion rates, the author argues for an approach driven by the principal value of developing independent learners. The disadvantages faced by distance educators in realizing this goal are examined, and the chapter concludes with an analysis of its implications for the respective roles of instructional design, course delivery and student-support services.

Only a few years ago, the very existence of open-learning institutions was considered a success. They provided unprecedented learning opportunities for a greater share of the populace, and enrolments grew much more quickly than had been anticipated. This pattern continues today in the developing world where the number of new open universities and the phenomenal numbers of students attending them are one of the most significant recent developments in higher education.

In more developed nations, however, these institutions are being subjected to considerably more scrutiny. The initial costs of establishing open universities are high, notably for course development, and governments are concerned about returns on their investments. Students, too, are becoming more discriminating consumers, and, whereas the initial intakes were grateful for the very existence of open-learning institutions, those in more recent intakes are concerned about high attrition rates and the difficulties of obtaining higher education in this way.

In response to such pressures for more accountability, it is important that institutional leaders develop clear criteria of success and tangible indicators with which to measure them, and that they ensure the development of a strong institutional ethos supported by management systems which ensure that these criteria are met.

In one sense, every course or programme completion is a success, given that most students in such institutions would not otherwise have had the opportunity to pursue a university education at all. From this perspective, it is not unreasonable to expect a higher attrition rate from open-learning institutions than from selective, campus-based ones. Nevertheless, especially in tighter fiscal climates, the funding sources for such institutions, mainly governments, are increasingly interested in and concerned about attrition and persistence indicators.

How then, in this environment, can one best measure the success of an open-learning institution?

Measures of success

There are a number of indicators available against which to evaluate open-learning institutions, the most common of which are:

- *completion rates:* the proportion of students who complete courses in which they are registered;
- *graduation rates:* the proportion of students who attain the formal academic credentials which they seek (although not necessarily from the initial institution);
- *persistence rates:* the proportion of students who take another course or courses after successfully completing the first one(s);
- *measures of cost efficiency and effectiveness:* the cost per course, per completion and per graduate.

Two other indicators, much more difficult to measure and yet nevertheless integral to the discussion below, are:

- *skill development:* the degree to which students develop their independent learning skills so that they can increasingly take responsibility for their own learning;
- *postgraduation performance:* the performance of graduates of open-learning programmes in subsequent education or employment.

These last two criteria of success measure aspects of the students' effectiveness as independent learners, a theme explored in some detail later in this chapter.

Perhaps the most frequently cited measure of success for open-learning institutions is the completion rate for courses delivered at a distance, especially given the variations in course-delivery modes across institutions. There is a growing body of research on this topic. One of the great difficulties is establishing what seems to be a reasonable rate of success, given that the institutions are typically nonselective (open admissions), that students may often proceed at their own pace, and that many of the entering students may derive what they wish from a particular course without necessarily completing all its assignments or a final examination. Nevertheless, within this sort of qualification, completion rates are the subject of considerable scrutiny among such institutions, and there is widespread agreement that they are too low (frequently less than 50 per cent of entrants complete their first course).

Cross-institutional comparison is extremely difficult, a point underlined very effectively by Shale,[1] who contrasts the different ways in which institutions calculate completion rates. He introduces the concept of 'nonstarters', students who entrol in a course but never subsequently participate in it. In an Athabasca University study conducted with 1978 and 1979 intakes, he found that fully half of the students were in this category.[2] He also pointed out the dramatic differences in course-completion rates if, on the one hand, one derived them from all students who originally enrolled in a course, or, on the other hand, computed them only after eliminating the nonstarters from the sample – in one case, the course-completion rate was 28.8 per cent for all who originally enrolled in a course, but 58.8 per cent if those classified as early withdrawals were removed from the calculations; in another, a completion rate of 70 per cent at the British Open University would be only 36 per cent if its initial screening mechanisms were taken into account.[3] There is even a self-selecting aspect to the latter – some of the OU students have to wait over a year to gain admission, and many, presumably including those who are less highly motivated, withdraw before their place becomes available, a fact which increases the proportion likely to succeed of those who do wait for a place.

Shale's finding was of more than mathematical significance. It suggested that there were at least two kinds of students enrolling in the university – those who were quite comfortable and successful with independent modes of learning and a very significant group who apparently were completely unprepared for this environment. This matches Moore's observation of three types of adult learner in distance education – those whom he labels 'self-directed learners', those who are self-directed in pursuit of credentials only, and those who have an emotional need for dependence.[4]

Such a high 'non-start' rate at Athabasca focused university attention on why so many students abandoned their studies almost before beginning them, and a number of contributing factors were identified. It was not difficult to discover that far too many were poorly informed about what they were in for and had little awareness of how to cope with the quite typical difficulties faced by home-study students in time management and self-motivation. The difficulties included having to work independently without the support of fellow students, working in nonsupportive home environments, or simply lacking the basic skills (reading, writing, mathematical, and study skills) to cope with the quantity and levels of work expected.

As a result, the university invested more resources into student information and support services, including the development of more local services through a regional office network, special workshops in study skills and examination writing, literacy and numeracy testing and referrals, better course-information outlines (available on-line), local on-line admission and registration, in-person seminars and workshops, and better career counselling. Attention was also paid to the design of courses with low completion rates and to ensuring that first units, in particular, were clear, relatively easy and provided immediate feedback to the student. Finally, attempts were made to encourage telephone tutors to be more active in initiating contacts with the student, especially those who seemed to be falling behind in the course, and telephone quizzes administered by tutors were built into the design of many courses to ensure student–tutor interaction during the course.

In 1988, the focus was sharpened further by building specific and ambitious completion- and persistence-rate targets over a five-year period right into Athabasca's Strategic Academic Plan. This, in turn, directed energies towards a whole series of measures such as improving the quality of service, response time, course design, student-support services and modes of delivery. While this action had the desired result of refocusing university attention on the performance of its students, it was not without its pitfalls.

Faculty tend to be suspicious of anything which can be portrayed as undermining academic standards. Obviously, completion rates could be increased simply by making the courses easier or marking more generously on final examinations. Another factor was the self-paced nature of AU courses, for research evidence is quite conclusive that institutional pacing increases completion rates.[5] However, the university's commitment to self-pacing is a deliberate one derived from the recognition that this 'open' dimension is critical to many of its students, who would otherwise be unable to follow a course which required them to stick to an imposed schedule. The completion-rate targets could also be achieved by an undue narrowing of focus; for example, by 'teaching to the examinations' and encouraging the sort of one-way rote learning to which distance learning is already so susceptible.

On balance, however, the decision was made to err on the side of paying too much attention to completion and persistence rates. It is all too easy to rationalize low completion rates away – 'What do you expect from open admissions?' or 'Our students aren't interested in course completion – they are taking the courses for interest only and don't necessarily have to write the final exam to derive what they want from the course.' The latter assertion was a common response at Athabasca University until a survey showed clearly that student completions were falling far short of even their own expectations – at the moment of admission, students expected to complete many more courses than they actually did, suggesting a large gap between their original expectations and their actual AU experience.[6]*

The commitment to measurable improvement in completion and persistence rates underlines the university's belief that the great majority of adult students are capable of successfully completing a university degree and that it has a responsibility to help them to achieve it.

While there has been a steady, if slow improvement in the university's completion rates over the past decade, it is very difficult to demonstrate a cause-and-effect relationship among the many and complex variables which affect it. Brindley's study[7] of attrition rates at the university provides an interesting perspective on this. Using a 'critical-incidents' technique whereby students identified factors which had facilitated or hindered their ability to complete a course, she found that course completers reported about the same number of 'hindering factors' (3.8) as did those who did not complete the course (3.7), and only a few more 'facilitating factors' (3.3 for completers to 2.5 reported by non-completers).[8] Hence, she concluded that differences between success and failure had more to do with the students' ability to cope with problems than did variations in their learning environment. This is echoed in Brookfield's finding that independent learners considered problems encountered in study not as blocks to progress but as the focus for effort.[9]

This suggests that there are strong personal variables which transcend the levels of support the institution offers and which are critical to determining whether or not someone will drop out of a course. In other words, it was not that students who dropped out faced any more hindering factors than did successful students, but that they were not able to cope with them as effectively as were the latter. Rather than concluding from this that student-support services are less critical than previously imagined, however, it directs attention to a new role – identifying students less well prepared for independent study and helping them to learn 'coping strategies' with which to overcome the typical and common barriers faced by home-study students.

*An effective institutional studies unit is invaluable in confronting the myths which every university develops. It can sometimes be very threatening, notably when it contradicts the senior manager's own misconceptions, but it is ultimately a key tool in keeping abreast of what is happening in the institution and as an objective check against internal perceptions of reality.

Towards a new measure of success: developing independent learners[10]

Standard completion and persistence rates are useful measures of an open university's productivity, but, it is argued below, the higher-order achievement of producing independent, self-directed learners is ultimately a more important criterion of institutional success. Given how little we still know about how people learn, and the difficulties faced by educators in even the most ideal learning environments in encouraging learner autonomy and independence, why should this be a central goal of open-learning institutions? There are a number of reasons for this position:

- The concept is central to the philosophy of open learning and adult education; this is, the importance of developing (as opposed to merely serving) 'self-actualized' learners.[11]
- Whereas initially, open-learning institutions provided opportunities for independent learners who lacked the formal qualifications or availability to attend conventional colleges and universities, they are increasingly serving a broader cross-section of the population, including many who would not previously have contemplated independent learning. This is even more the case in the developing world, where distance education has become a primary response to mass demands for higher education and mainly serves the 18–24 year-old age group.[12]
- There is an economic argument, on the assumption that relatively autonomous learners make fewer demands for instructional support and services than do more dependent students. They may complete courses and programmes more quickly and require less tutorial and counselling help. If the ideal student is one who ultimately outgrows his or her teacher, the ideal open university is one which breeds students who no longer require its support.
- Tait[13] has expressed concern about the susceptibility of distance education to totalitarian control, with some institutions being established deliberately to avoid creating conventional campuses, which are seen as breeding grounds for student radicalism. This gives additional meaning to Chesterton's[14] emphasis on the continuing responsibility of distance educators to pay close attention to the values and assumptions which their courses transmit, to find ways to give students more curriculum control, and to induce them to challenge what they learn.
- Most fundamentally in a 'knowledge' society, one that is constantly facing discontinuous change, all educational institutions have a responsibility to induce learners to challenge the nature of knowledge,

to question and requestion everything they 'learn', and to strive for the ideals of reflection and *praxis* set out by writers like Paulo Friere.[15] For an excellent series of articles in this domain, the reader is referred to the recent book edited by Terry Evans and Daryl Nation, *Critical Reflections on Distance Education.*[16]

The concept of an independent learner is not an absolute one, but a notion that graduates should be more 'self-sufficient' learners than they were at the point of entry. It involves changes in personal values (openness to new ideas and to rethinking current beliefs) and attitudes (self-motivation), as well as the development of new skills (time management, study skills, problem conceptualization, critical and lateral thinking, and research and library skills). A quest never completely fulfilled, it is a process central to the concepts of open learning and lifelong education.

By contrast, the dependent learner is more likely to want to be told what to learn and how to learn it and less apt to go beyond the minimum demands of a particular assignment to challenge its usefulness or to apply what has been learned more broadly or personally. The essential difference, following Dewey and Whitehead and as discussed by Boot and Hodgson,[17] is between knowledge as a process and knowledge as a commodity. This point has been underlined by Mary Thorpe:

> We should begin from the assumption that course materials are not the course; rather that the course is an annual process of interaction between students, the materials and the tutors and that, in this sense, tutors and students 'produce' courses as well as course teams.[18]

Until recently, open universities have been catering primarily to a population not otherwise served by formal educational institutions. Previously, many strong-willed people with a capacity for independent learning were denied access to college or university by rigid entrance requirements, costs, time constraints and enrolment quotas, all of which have been reduced or eliminated by the advent of open universities. Such individuals have been well served by these innovative institutions, but the latter have also benefited from such self-directed students who have succeeded while making minimal demands for guidance and service.

The principal argument here is that much of the success of open-learning institutions has been the product of independent learners who would succeed in almost any system. If they are truly to live up to the potential suggested by their ideals, and especially as they are confronted with new groups of students less well prepared for independent study, open-learning institutions must improve their capacity to develop independent learners, a criterion much more difficult to measure than course completion or graduation rates.

The issue has been given a lot of attention in the literature of distance education and open learning, notably by Brookfield,[19] Burge,[20] Gibbs,[21] Higgs,[22] Inglis,[23] Kelly and Shapcott,[24] Moore,[25] Morgan,[26] and Wickett,[27] but there is very little substantial evidence to date that products of such institutions are more autonomous, independent or self-directed as learners than they were at the point of entry. Before too much is made of this, however, it is pertinent to look at such attempts in supposedly more advantaged domains.

On conventional university campuses, students may or may not be encouraged to develop their independent learning skills. All too commonly, education is treated as the dissemination and repetition-on-demand of a fixed, unchanging entity called 'knowledge'. This is most prevalent where students sit in large lecture halls, take broad survey courses examined mainly by multiple-choice tests, or learn to 'case' (ie learn to predict) examination questions and are rewarded for regurgitating lecture notes on the finals.

On the other hand, on-campus students may be encouraged to move quite dramatically along the dependent-independent continuum. An inspiring lecturer, a stimulating discussion or reading, or, as is so often the case, serendipitous exposure to the ideas of fellow students may motivate the student to pursue a particular issue in depth, way beyond the demands of a course. This, in turn, will require the development of research skills and may inspire new interests which change the way the student looks at the world. For on-campus students, the interactive atmosphere and freedom of full-time study may be very stimulating in changing their attitudes towards and capacity for learning.

Do open universities do more to promote independent learners than campus-based ones? Other than providing more opportunities for adult and part-time learners, they may do less, notably where their primary mode of delivery is through home study and distance education. For example:

- As Chesterton[28] has observed, the separation of teacher and learner and the production of prepackaged materials in distance education shifts the focus of curriculum decision-making away from the students and more towards the institution and its staff. This is supported by Millard[29] in a critique of what he sees to be a tendency at the British Open University to take decisions for administrative convenience rather than educational effectiveness.
- The prepackaged course materials, especially if handsomely printed and bound, may carry undue authority for many students, who are consequently less apt to challenge what they have learned.[30]

- Because they are highly visible to academic peers as well as to students, courses tend to be overly heavy in content. This may also encourage students to focus on digesting the content rather than on its meaning and application.
- Courses tend to be built around prescribed and supplementary reference materials. While this is logical for and helpful to isolated home-study students, it does not encourage them to search out their own sources or to develop library skills.
- A centrally produced package of course materials 'cannot admit of the infinite variety of advice and support that is demanded by learners'[31] and makes little provision for their individual differences in backgrounds, needs and learning styles.
- While most open universities provide access to tutors and even seminars in support of home-study courses, students usually lack the immediacy of feedback that comes from more regular and concentrated interaction with other students and staff, and hence are less apt to develop the inclination to challenge or question what they need. Harris[32] has been a particularly effective critic of the student passivity which can follow undue reliance on prepackaged materials.

In attempts to overcome these weaknesses by emulating support offered on traditional campuses, many open universities have added a wide range of services and delivery modes which provide increased interaction with staff and other students. However, because so little is known about how people learn and because of the overwhelming influence of personal, as opposed to institutional, factors on a student's performance,[33] the result is often a roulette game, an expensive hit-or-miss approach with marginal impact on completion rates and increased costs per student.

Before pursuing the problem of how an open university can develop independent learners, it is important to look more directly at the problem students face in coping with the demands of open learning.

Open-university students and the problems they face

At least until recently, demographic profiles of students in open-learning institutions have been remarkably consistent. Whether part-time or full-time, they are working adults and homemakers, the majority aged between 25 and 40.[34] While much has been written about the 'self-actualized' adult learner,[35] many are returning to formal education for the first time in years, often with negative previous experiences. I have written elsewhere[36] about the 'myth' of the self-actualized learner, and the large number of students who do not cope effectively with the demands for independence, time management and self-direction posed by open learning.

If open universities are to be successful in developing independent learning, they must do a great deal more than has usually been done to address that objective. Too often, their policies and practices have worked actively against it. One example is the way in which such institutions are usually promoted, stressing convenience and flexibility rather than the difficulties faced by most students. Responding to such slogans as 'stay home and go to university' or 'give yourself credit', many who have finally mustered up the courage to enrol after some years' absence from formal education find themselves totally unprepared for its demands. While one cannot expect an institution to say, 'earn your degree the slow and painful way', it is important that incoming students are made fully aware of the challenges they will face.

Experience has suggested that such students tend to blame themselves rather than the university for their failures. Fage and Mills[37] have noted that Open University students seldom complain if they are not happy with a course, while I have observed the same tendency at Athabasca University.[38] This reinforces the notion that developing an adult student's self-confidence is the first challenge for an open university. This has implications for such services as the registrar's office and student services, normally the first contact points for students; for the training of course tutors; for the design of foundation or introductory courses; and for student information and orientation services.

One of the biggest problems faced by first-time students in such an environment is the absence of peers. While this is a serious academic problem, given the importance of interaction and being exposed to different perspectives on issues, it is even more fundamental a concern in terms of student persistence.

On a university campus, if a new student finds a lecture incomprehensible or boring, he or she can check this perception immediately with fellow students. It is easy to forget how reassuring and supportive it is to learn that others found the material or the lecturer just as difficult to understand as we did. If there is no one else to talk to, students will be more apt to blame themselves, assume that they are 'just not up' to that level of work, and drop out without sharing their concerns. This is a major challenge when students are separated from the institution and from each other by what Moore calls 'transactional distance'.[39] Open universities thus have a responsibility to do whatever they can to put students in contact with each other, and to allow them success which they can build upon as they gain confidence in their own ability to do university-level work.

One variable which appears to be useful in determining success is that of choice – whether or not the student actively chooses an open-learning institution over conventional alternatives. At Athabasca University, there has been a rural/urban dimension to this. Many urban students actively select AU over campus-based alternatives because they prefer the independence and flexibility it offers, whereas most rural students have no other choice if they are not prepared or cannot afford to move to the nearest university town.

AU's experience has been that rural students are more demanding of social interaction – they are more apt to want a professor in the class-room, and to debate issues with their peers. If they cannot have this on a regular basis in their own community, they at least want teleconfer-enced seminars or computer conferencing – anything which will offer them an alternative to trying to work through the materials in isolation. This experience is apparently replicated in Yugoslavia, where Krajnc found great differences between those who *chose* to study at a distance and those who had no other option.[40] The latter had a more negative view of distance education, much less readiness to adapt to new methods of learning, and a greater tendency to seek interaction and socialization.[41]

Krajnc argues that the development of initial student expectations for independent and self-directed learning will contribute considerably to positive outcomes even in isolated rural settings.[42] She also notes the irony that, while students with a lower self-esteem are those most likely to have difficulty with independent learning, they are also the group most apt to choose distance education courses (out of the false impres-sion that they are less demanding than classroom-based ones).[43]

Finally, Krajnc makes an interesting distinction between 'ex-troverted' and 'introverted' learners, as distinguished by their desire for and effectiveness in social interaction and 'functioning in front of others', concluding that:

> Both extreme sub-groups of learners (those wit'. extremely low sociabil-ity and those with extremely high sociability) do not function favourably in distance education in social isolation.[44]

In other words, the extreme extroverts require more social interaction than independent learning offers, while the extreme introverts require the stimulation and motivation which interactive learning situations provide. This is an interesting response to Masson's hypothesis that distance education is better suited to introverts than to extroverts.[45]

In summary, with more and more students with different needs and learning styles enrolling, it is incumbent upon open-learning institutions to do more than merely provide access to higher education.

Institutional responses to student concerns: a critical perspective

Institutions have responded to the needs of part-time adult learners in three major areas – instructional design, course-delivery systems and student-support services. One major difficulty is that these have usually been addressed in a piecemeal fashion, often by separate functional departments in the university – an instructional-design/course-development unit; a tutorial-services/course-delivery or presentation unit; and a student-services unit. One of the important functions of a strong strategic plan (discussed in Chapter 10) is to integrate these services into a comprehensive and coherent whole focusing on the needs of the student.

INSTRUCTIONAL-SYSTEMS DESIGN

In the 'industrial' model of course production, which has been the dominant approach in distance education, instructional designers are an integral part of a course team. Usually behaviourist in training, their function is to ensure that the materials are broken down into learning units with clear objectives and subobjectives, with students often proceeding on a 'mastery-learning model' until each unit has been completed. The more extreme practitioners of this art have even suggested an ideal of 'teacher-proof' courses, ones so well designed that students are better off without the assistance of a teacher or tutor.

Whatever its limitations, and these are explored further below, instructional design has been an important component in the success of distance education. Home study is difficult enough for students without their being confronted with badly written or poorly designed courses or thick textbooks which they are supposed to read and understand on their own. Moreover, university academics, knowing that their courses are going to be open to public scrutiny, may overload their courses, both in terms of volume and level of academic work, to ensure their academic credibility with professional peers, and it is very useful to have an instructional designer and editor there to check this tendency and to serve as student advocates in the preparation of course materials (even though they seldom have direct contact with the students themselves).

In practice, while course-team interaction can be very stimulating and productive, it is also time-consuming and may sometimes produce bad compromises rather than a good resolution of the inevitable conflicts that arise among any group of academics. There is also the danger noted by Farnes[46] that the course-team experience may be more stimulating and exciting than the actual course which results so that it is the staff rather than the students who derive the most benefit from the exercise.

The concept of a teacher-proof course also ignores the different needs of different groups of learners. A teacher or tutor is there to mediate between the course and the learner, to help the latter to adapt and apply materials to his or her own purposes and contexts. In their deliberations on the design of the Dutch Open University, Chang et al advocated a number of interactive learning systems to compensate for the limitations of written instruction.[47]

With its emphasis on measurable objectives and mastery learning, instructional-systems design has also proven to be an effective approach to computer-assisted learning and to in-service training. It appears to be particularly well suited to teaching specific procedures, physical tasks or sequential concepts, and there are many examples of its successful adaptation. However, central as it has been to the development of distance education, there is increasing concern about the theoretical basis for this approach and its impact on student learning. One of the most important and well-researched critiques, emanating from Britain's Open University, which pioneered approaches to instruction developed by educational technologists, is that of David Harris.[48]

Harris wonders whether the actual practice of open learning is as open as is usually supposed. He associates the instructional designer's process of simplifying, clarifying and organizing the text with 'closing' it as well, resulting in a 'hidden curriculum' which arises from the 'unstated but powerful and often highly conventional expectations of pupils or colleagues in practice'.[49] He urges educators to look at openness not just in abstract terms, but in micropolitical ones – what actually happens? How do learners use the materials? Who has the power?[50]

The Open University has attempted to counter the worst excesses of a 'teachist' approach to education through its strong regional networks; foundation courses, which look at personal as well as intellectual development; and compulsory summer-school sessions, which provide the sorts of interaction, personal support and challenges to rote learning which otherwise might be missing. Current ICDE president David Sewart, through both his writings[51] and his actions as director of Regional Academic Services, has been a major force in these developments.

More recently, the Evans and Nation book, *Critical Reflections on Distance Education*,[52] goes much further in challenging the dominant place of what the editors term the 'instructional technologist' approach to distance education. In their 'critical reflections', the editors are concerned that students are treated passively as 'objects' in such systems, and that these systems impose bureaucratic structures on 'teachers' which severely limit their ability to induce students to take responsibility for and to challenge their own learning.

> The separation of teacher and student, the disempowerment of students
> from making decisions about their own learning, the requirements of pro-
> duction schedules, postal dispatches and the many other aspects of
> working education, spin an intricate web around the teacher in distance
> education.[53]

Evans and Nation and their colleagues have produced a refreshing and
extremely welcome volume in its concern for the quality of the learning
experience of distance students and its candour in confronting the challenges and problems this mode of education faces.

Even where criticism of educational technological approaches has
been less focused, almost all institutions using these techniques have
tried to compensate for them by offering more interactive modes of
instruction and support alongside the basic course package. Perhaps the
most notable has been the use of telephone and face-to-face tutors to
assist students in coping with the demands of centrally prepared home-
study courses, although, as discussed immediately below, there are
often severe limitations on the tutor's authority, and there can be much
confusion about his or her role *vis-à-vis* the built-in instructional design.
It should also be admitted that the motivation for supplementing and
complementing course packages has come more from concerns about
high student-attrition rates than intrinsic commitments to developing
independent and self-directed learners.

COURSE-DELIVERY SYSTEMS

While thoroughly and slickly prepared course materials did much to
promote distance learning in the early days, it was quickly evident that
many part-time adult students needed a lot more personal and academic
support than that provided by the traditional correspondence mode of
delivery. Students who had not engaged in formal learning for some
time, many of whom had doubts about their own learning abilities, were
expected to be strongly self-motivated, to have excellent time-management and study skills and to perform a great deal of reading and writing
in their own time with a minimum of guidance and feedback.

In response, mainly because of very low completion rates among first-
time students, universities have developed much more sophisticated
and extensive support services and further enhancements to the basic
course-delivery model. In more densely populated areas, such as
Europe, open universities have offered regular in-person tutorials at
regional or local centres (the British Open University has 13 regional
centres, each of which is served by from 10 to 20 'study' centres, most
within 50 miles of the majority of its students). In more sparsely
populated regions, such as in Canada and Australia, in-person seminars

have been supplemented by telephone tutoring, seminars linking various groups by telephone via a teleconferencing 'bridge', and various models of computer-assisted learning.

Moreover, universities are increasingly patterning their course delivery to the needs of special groups. At Athabasca, for instance, on-site full-time teaching, with strong local counselling and advising support, is offered in several native study centres to respond to the particular needs of the local culture in each case. A similar scheme is in operation in a number of federal penitentiaries. In providing upgrading and degree and certificate programmes to employees of major corporations, the university often offers classes on site in the company with students pursuing the materials in their own time at home.

A recent and exciting innovation, in process at Athabasca and at the Open University of British Columbia, is the 'capstone' programme, whereby university courses, still relying on the basic course packages, are offered on college campuses to allow graduates of the two-year 'university transfer' programmes in the colleges to complete their university degree while staying in their own community. The courses are taught, often by the community-college instructors themselves, with the support of such local facilities as the registrar's office, library and student-services units. The university retains control of quality by hiring the instructors, monitoring the curriculum through its course packages, and setting and marking the final examinations. While not 'distance education' in its purest sense, this is a progressive step towards the achievement of the goals of open learning, as many of the students would otherwise have to leave their community to attend university – even if they could secure a place in a campus-based institution in another town, they probably could not afford the additional living expenses.

Again, the idea is an excellent one but its implementation poses a number of issues for management. In fact, the quality-control measures cited above pose a number of contradictions between the dual needs of central control and local adaptation.

As noted above, instructional designers tend to design the courses so that they stand on their own. In this conception, a tutor's role is merely to assist the student to understand the basic design of the course and to work through it, primarily independently. In practice, however, universities tend to hire well-qualified tutors (usually with at least a master's degree in the relevant discipline) to protect their academic integrity. The result is often an instructor who is too well-qualified to serve merely as a facilitating agent. A good tutor will want to adapt the materials to local needs, to introduce new materials and to 'teach' the students in ways not originally envisioned by the course design. This can cause problems, both for the implementation of the course and for the role of the tutor.

This problem is exacerbated by the common tendency of such institutions to set independently marked central examinations. An understandable practice, given concerns about academic standards in such a loose and widespread organization, this can be extremely frustrating for tutors and students alike if the final examination doesn't reflect local issues or a particular slant on the course offered by the tutor. One solution is to give the tutors some control over final examination questions, and hence to encourage rather than frustrate their attempts to make the materials meaningful to the local student group.

Research by Bagley and Challis[54] underlines the difficulties faced by tutors in open-learning systems. If the courses are very flexible, and students are self-paced and start at different times, the tutor must be able to respond to questions on all aspects of the course at any given moment (as opposed to the university lecturer who can prepare for each individual class knowing that all students are at the same point in the course). They found that faculty participating in open-learning schemes frequently had difficulty in adjusting to threats to the control they were used to in the classroom – control over content, over pacing and, to a considerable degree, over what and how the student learns. They found role confusion and ambivalence towards the whole question of student autonomy.

A particular dimension of this conflict was that between the teacher's commitment to the notion of the self-actualized adult student who takes full responsibility for his or her learning and a natural feeling of responsibility for the student's success or failure. Open-learning institutions are always having to make compromises on this score, sometimes for fiscal reasons and sometimes in recognition that even (or especially?) adult students need support and direction if they are to succeed.

As Bagley and Challis express it:

> It is, on the surface, much easier to grant adult students the right to autonomy but if that student is entering, or re-entering, the learning situation with trepidation and perhaps with some learning difficulties, the conscientious teacher is likely to feel no less concern.[55]

Athabasca University confronted this problem recently in tightening up what had been a very liberal policy enabling students to suspend study for extensive periods without cost or penalty. This had been cited as a keystone of the university's flexibility in ensuring that such student problems as a temporary illness, responsibilities to an employer for a conference or short-term project, or a farmer's need to bring in the harvest did not prevent the student from pursuing the course. On the other side of the ledger, this practice was tying up a lot of resources, notably tutors thus not available to other students, and it was found that very few students who suspended study ever completed the course. Hence, it was replaced by a policy which allowed students to extend studies for three months for an additional fee, although there was also unofficial provision for exceptions under compelling circumstances.

STUDENT-SUPPORT SERVICES

The persistence of high attrition rates, despite revisions in course design and delivery, has led many researchers to identify 'personal' (as opposed to 'institutional') factors as essential to understanding why students have difficulty in pursuing education at a distance. Continuing high attrition, despite improvements in support services, has led to a greater emphasis on pre-admission services, which are intended to evaluate readiness of the student to learn via home study without reneging on the institution's commitment to open admissions. Hence, while students are not denied access to the institution, a lot more attention is paid to what they will need in order to succeed, to prevent the open door from being a revolving one.[56]

Imaginative and effective orientation, information, and counselling and advising programmes have been developed which enable students to test their basic skills, motivation and intentions against the provision of and demands made by distance-education programmes. These pre-admission programmes have met with considerable success, but they introduce new costs, may not be universally accessible, and, being more in the affective domain, may not have as much political support within the university as do more 'cerebral' matters such as academic programmes or more money for research.

An institution's commitment to strong student services is critical to the fundamental value of opening up access to a university education. It is one of the critical tests of the extent to which resource allocation and decision-making are based on a value-driven approach or a more political one, as described in my contribution to the 1988 ICDE Conference in Oslo.[57]

To succeed in an independent-study environment, a student needs to be very clear about his or her learning objectives; to have effective reading, writing, study and time-management skills; and to have a strong sense of self and the motivation requisite to overcoming the inevitable barriers to success such as competing priorities, lack of interaction with peers and a less than ideal environment for study. The ultimate challenge is not only to provide such services when students need them, but to develop each student's capacity to look after his or her own learning needs.

As institutions committed to lifelong learning, open universities must do more than provide access and support. In every day, in every way, they must be passionate advocates of lifelong learning and do everything they can to help their students develop the attitudes and skills which will maximize their opportunities for it.

The development of independent learning as a fundamental institutional value

In this chapter, the case for the development of independent learning as a fundamental institutional value and hence as a measure of its success has been advocated. This is not to suggest that such indicators as completion and persistence rates and costs per completion or cost per graduate should be abandoned, for both institutions and governments will always need such basic data to assess their effectiveness. Instead, the call here is for a higher-order objective, one which will provide leadership for all levels and types of education.

The dice may be loaded against the development of independent learners, but this is no excuse not to pursue this ideal thoroughly and aggressively. The starting point is to instil this commitment as a value fundamental to the direction and management of the institution and hence to address a number of key issues from this perspective.

Moore[58] has offered an interesting starting point, offering three major implications of such a commitment – training tutors and course writers in self-directed learning, offering student-support services on a demand-only basis, and decoupling the teaching function from the accreditation function. Morrison[59] has taken up the latter point and challenged the whole notion of university accreditation in looking to the future of postsecondary education.

Evans and Nation[60] have criticized the instructional industrialists for their failure to recognize and encourage the autonomy of adults in their own learning, and decried the conservative and passive nature of our institutions:

> Distance education uses its textual, curricular and pedagogical processes to marginalize and dissolve the self-directedness of people's learning, and confines them to a system of learning which reflects and aids the reproduction of the ideological and structural conditions of society.[61]

Whether or not these perspectives and objectives are realistic and feasible, they are stimulating challenges to the whole way we view and evaluate our open universities. As a process, they combat smugness and complacency and force those of us working in such institutions to question what we take for granted, to live up to our ideals, and to provide the kinds of learning institutions which not only meet the needs of incoming students but also challenge them to develop themselves in ways they had never previously envisioned. In the process, it is inevitable that the same thing will happen to us, the staff members of such institutions.

Whether or not we choose to try to measure the extent to which our graduates have become independent learners, our institutions are being judged informally on this basis every day – by graduate schools and by employers who are still not very knowledgeable about what open-learning institutions are and how to evaluate their products. In the short run, we are doing well, because our earlier graduates were, almost by definition, already independent learners, but the real proof is in what happens from now on as we attract more and more traditional learners, many just out of secondary school.

Notes

1. Shale, D G (1982), 'Attrition: A Case Study' in Daniel, Stroud and Thompson (eds), *Learning at a Distance: A World Perspective,* Edmonton: Athabasca University, pp 113–17.
2. Ibid, p 115.
3. Ibid, pp 115, 117.
4. Moore, M (1986), 'Self-Directed Learning and Distance Education', *Journal of Distance Education,* I (1), Autumn, p 12.
5. See, for example, Coldeway, Dan (1982), 'Recent Research in Distance Learning' in Daniel, J S, Stroud, M R and Thompson, J A, *Learning at a Distance: A World Perspective,* Edmonton: Athabasca University, p 33.
6. Conway, C and Powell, R (1986), 'An Analysis of AU Students; Motivators, Intentions and Behaviour', Athabasca: Centre for Distance Education, 11 June.
7. Brindley, Jane E (1988), 'A Model of Attrition for Distance Education' in Sewart and Daniel (eds), *Developing Distance Education,* Oslo: ICDE, pp 131–7.
8. Ibid, p 135.
9. Brookfield, S (1982), 'Independent Learners and Correspondence Students', *Teaching at a Distance,* 22, p 26.
10. An earlier version of this section appeared recently in *Open Learning* – Paul, R H (1990), 'Towards a New Measure of Success: Developing Independent Learners', *Open Learning,* 4 (3), Feb, pp 37–44. Moreover, some of the material is taken directly from Paul, R H (1989), 'Do Open Universities Do a Better Job of Developing

Independent Learners?' in Tait, A (ed), *Interaction and Independence: Student Support in Distance Education and Open Learning,* conference papers for the ICDE/UKOU Conference at Downing College, Cambridge, Sept 19–22, pp 182–93.

11. Knowles, M (1973), *Self-Directed Learning: A Guide for Learners and Teachers,* New York: Association Press.
12. Daniel, J S (1989), 'Interaction and Independence: How is the Mixture Changing?' in Tait, A, op cit, p 63.
13. Tait, A (1989), 'Democracy and Distance Education: The Role of Tutorial and Counselling services', *Journal of Distance Education,* 3 (1), pp 95–9.
14. Chesterton, P (1985), 'Curriculum Control in Distance Education', *Teaching at a Distance,* 1 (26), p 32.
15. Friere, P (1970), *Pedagogy of the Oppressed,* New York: Continuum.
16. Evans, T and Nation, D (eds), (1989), *Critical Reflections on Distance Education,* London: Falmer Press.
17. Boot, R L and Hodgson, V E (1987), 'Open Learning: Meaning and Experience' in Hodgson, V E et al (eds), *Beyond Distance Teaching – Towards Open Learning,* Milton Keynes: Open University Press.
18. Thorpe, M (1979), 'When is a Course Not a Course?' *Teaching at a Distance,* 16, p 13.
19. Brookfield, S (1982), 'Independent Learners and Correspondence Students', *Teaching at a Distance,* 22, p 26.
20. Burge, E (1988), 'Beyond Andragogy: Some Explorations for Distance Learning Design', *Journal of Distance Education,* 3 (1), pp 5–23.
21. Gibbs, G (1984), 'Learning to Learn – the Student-Centred Approach' in Henderson, E S and Nathenson, M B (eds), *Independent Learning in Higher Education,* Englewood Cliffs, New Jersey: Educational Technology Publications.
22. Higgs, J. (1988), 'Planning Learning Experiences to Promote Autonomous Learning' in Boud, E (ed), *Developing Student Autonomy in Learning,* London: Kogan Page, ch 2, pp 40–58.
23. Inglis, P (1989), 'Supporting Learning at a Distance: External Students' Perceptions of the Contribution and Importance of Certain Teaching and Learning Conditions to their Development of Learning Independence, with Particular Reference to the Affective Domain', unpublished thesis submitted in partial fulfilment of the doctor of philosophy degree, University of Queensland, Australia.
24. Kelly, M and Shapcott, M (1985), 'Approaches to Learning: Understanding the Adult Learner', ICDE Conference, Melbourne, Australia, no 1260.

25. Moore, M (1986), 'Self-directed Learning and Distance Education', *Journal of Distance Education,* 1 (1), pp 7–24.
26. Morgan, A (1985), 'What Shall We Do about Independent Learning?', *Teaching at a Distance,* 26, pp 38–45.
27. Wickett, R (1986), 'Models for Independent Learning: Applications for Distance Education', *Open Campus,* 12, pp 27–33.
28. Chesterton, P (1985), 'Curriculum Control in Distance Education', *Teaching at a Distance,* 26, p 32.
29. Millard, J (1985), 'Local Tutor–Student contact in the Open University', *Teaching at a Distance,* 26, p 11.
30. Wolfe, R and Murgatroyd, S (1979), 'The Open University and the Negotiation of Knowledge', *Higher Education Review,* 11 (2), pp 9–16.
31. Sewart, D (1989), 'Interaction Costs Money, Independence is Free?' in A Tait (ed), *Interaction and Independence: Student Support in Distance Education and Open Learning,* papers for ICDE/UKOU Conference, Downing College, Cambridge, pp 251–6.
32. Harris, D (1987), *Openness and Closure in Distance Education,* Lewes: Falmer Press, pp 139–42.
33. Brindley, J E (1988), 'A Model of Attrition for Distance Education' in Sewart, D and Daniel, J S (eds), *Developing Distance Education,* Oslo: ICDE, pp 131–7.
34. For example, the author's review of the demographic patterns of students at Canada's three open universities revealed remarkably similar data. See Paul, R (1989), 'Canada's Open Universities: Issues and Prospectives' in Sweet R (ed), *Post-Secondary Distance Education in Canada,* Athabasca: Athabasca University and the Canadian Society for Studies in Education, p 146.
35. Notably Malcolm Knowles, op cit.
36. Paul, R H (1988), 'If Student Services Are So Important, Then Why Are We Cutting Them Back?' in Sewart, D and Daniel, J S, op cit, p 51.
37. Fage, J and Mills, R (1986), 'Student–Tutor Feedback in the Open University', *Open Learning,* 1 (3), p 44.
38. Paul, R H (1988), 'If Student Services Are So Important, Then Why Are We Cutting Them Back?' in Sewart, D. and Daniel, J S, op cit, p 51.
39. Moore, M (1983), 'The Individual Adult Learner' in Tight, M (ed), *Adult Learning and Education,* London: Croom Helm, pp 157–8.
40. Krajnc, A (1988), 'Social Isolation and Learning Effectiveness in Distance Education', *Ziff Papiere 71,* Hagen: Fernuniversität, p 5.
41. Ibid, p 15.
42. Ibid, p 10.

43. Ibid, p 20.
44. Ibid, p 35.
45. Masson, J (1987), 'La clientele étudiante et les institutions de formation à distance', *Journal of Distance Education,* 2 (fall), pp 55–64.
46. Farnes, M (1976), 'An Educational Technologist Looks at Student-Centred Learning', *British Journal of Educational Technology,* 7 (1).
47. Chang, T M et al (1983), *Distance Learning: On the Design of an Open University,* Boston, Mass: Kluwer-Nijhoff Publishing, ch 4.
48. Harris, D (1987), *Openness and Closure in Distance Education,* Lewes: Falmer Press.
49. Ibid, p 14.
50. Ibid, p 15.
51. Sewart, D (1982), 'Distance Teaching: A Contradiction in Terms?' in Sewart, D, Keegan, D, and Holmberg, B (eds), *Distance Education: International Perspectives,* London: Croom Helm, pp 46–61.
52. Evans and Nation, op cit.
53. Ibid, p 246.
54. Bagley, B and Challis, B (1985), *Inside Open Learning,* Coombe Lodge: Further Education Staff College, pp 58–64.
55. Ibid, pp 33–34.
56. Paul, R H (1989), 'Is the Open Door a Revolving Door? A Plea for Stronger Student Support in Distance Education', paper presented at ETIC '89, Birmingham, England, April (to be published in conference proceedings).
57. For an analysis of why student-services units face difficult political battles in their own institutions, see Paul, R H (1988), 'If Student Services Are So Important, Then Why Are We Cutting Them Back?' in Sewart and Daniel, *Developing Distance Education,* 1988, pp 50–6.
58. Moore, M (1986), 'Self-Directed Learning and Distance Education', *Journal of Distance Education,* 1, 1 (Autumn), pp 18–19.
59. Morrison, T (1989), 'Beyond Legitimacy: Facing the Future in Distance Education', *International Journal of Lifelong Education,* 8 (1), Jan–Mar, pp 3–24.
60. Evans and Nation, op cit, p 248.
61. Ibid, p 249.

CHAPTER 7

Managing at a Distance: Regional Networks and Off-Campus Tutors

Chapter synopsis

There are two particular management dilemmas which most sharply bring into play the difficulties of managing at a distance – the management and direction of regional offices located some distance from the central facility and the supervision and support of networks of part-time, off-campus tutors. Each of these is examined in turn, notably from the perspective of the political and value-driven forms of leadership described by Badaracco and Ellsworth.

Managing regional networks: centralization and decentralization

It is no accident that most of the world's open universities, especially those in the West, have developed major regional networks in support of their academic programmes. A regional network typically involves a series of local or regional offices, sometimes connected by computer systems, which offer a number of the institution's services on a more personal and local basis.

For example, Britain's Open University has 13 regional offices which provide such services as information and counselling, on-site seminars, and extensive local networks of tutors and tutor counsellors for academic support, advice and counselling in almost every region of England, Scotland, Wales and Northern Ireland. Athabasca University has three major regional offices which offer almost all of the university's student services in the local community – information, advising and counselling, on-line admissions and registration, course materials pick-up, examination supervision, seminars and teleconferencing, and financial aid, although most of these are also available by post and telephone

While they may offer some savings (for example, reduced postal and telephone charges), regional offices are mainly an 'add-on' expense.

That is, they are not strictly necessary to the functioning of the institution but represent a local presence and a 'human face'. In addition to the obvious and direct costs of leasing or purchasing facilities, staffing, and capital and operating costs, a regional network increases the complexity of communications and administration.

THE JUSTIFICATION FOR REGIONAL NETWORKS

What then is the justification for this added cost of course and programme delivery? Reasons vary with each institution, but the following would usually be cited:

- Whatever the advantages of distance education, service by post or telephone is seldom as effective or as personal as it is face-to-face. Hence, a major reason for regional offices is to provide local, personalized and more convenient service.
- Following from this, regional offices strengthen the local identity of the institution, especially if they are given some freedom to respond to local needs. However, this is sometimes more theoretical than real as open universities are often reluctant to permit very much local or regional variation in the form, content or evaluation of courses. (This issue is discussed in some detail below.)
- It follows that regional offices are an important marketing tool for the institution. In countries like Canada and Australia, where sparse populations are spread over great geographic distances, a regional centre is an important factor in a student's decision to study at and remain with an open university. It may be the only such institution within several hundred miles, and it thus takes on an identity it would never have otherwise. Notable examples are the regional centres of the Open University in Wales and Northern Ireland, and Athabasca's in Fort McMurray, Alberta.
- Local centres can greatly reduce the 'turnaround' time for such key student services as registration and course-materials pick-up, and paper and examination marking, speedier service being an important factor in student persistence and success.
- The institution is able to offer local supplementary services that enhance student support, such as study skills workshops, orientation sessions, and computer laboratories.
- Where courses are institutionally paced, as at Britain's Open University, regional and local operations provide an opportunity for classes to meet together on a regular basis. They can also host summer schools and weekend workshops.
- Regional and local centres can be used as meeting places to instil a stronger sense of identity among tutors and other part-time staff and

to bring central staff and governing boards into closer contact with students (most of whom never visit the main offices of an open university).

- While it is seldom cited as a reason for the creation of regional offices, one of their most valuable functions is to provide distance-learning institutions with direct, personal feedback on their performance. Students are usually more assertive about their concerns and rights when talking face-to-face to a university clerk or counsellor than they will be over the phone or by letter. The setting is also more conducive to an in-depth discussion of the particular problem or concern and how it can be resolved. Of course, it is one thing for the regional offices to get strong feedback from the university's customers/clients, and quite another for the intensity of that feedback to reach those in the central offices who are responsible for the various student services. Regional clerical staff can be as frustrated as the students themselves in trying to elicit responses from central authorities.

This frustration is often exacerbated by a lack of understanding or disagreement with centrally developed policies on the part of regional staff. With the different view of the institution which isolation from the main institution often develops, regional staff are more apt to see things the way students see them, and hence they are less able or willing to uphold institutional policy when students challenge it. They advance the cause of the institution if they are able to identify and change incomplete or inappropriate policy, but they undermine it if they challenge policies and procedures because they are ignorant of their rationales and wider implications.

CENTRALIZATION AND DECENTRALIZATION: A CLASSIC DILEMMA

Whatever their advantages, regional offices introduce major management problems for the institution. This is not unique to open learning, for centralized/decentralized conflicts are classic in the literature of organizational theory.

Brooke[1] likens centralized and decentralized approaches to management to the efficiency and size of supermarkets as compared to the friendliness of the corner shop. Centralization is intended to facilitate goal-setting and the consequent allocation of resources for the whole organization, encouraging clear direction, coherent goals and economies of scale. Decentralization adds the critical components of staff personal responsibility and ownership, quicker response to local demands, and a stronger loyalty to the organization. Presumably, the goal of any service organization, including an open university, is to is to find an appropriate balance between the two and the advantages of both.

This is easier said than done. Brooke writes of the endless cycles of organizational tinkering associated with trying to get the mixture right. The first of his four propositions about this issue is

that organizations waste resources (human and material) by adopting a cycle of change between centralization and autonomy; good reasons are given for the changes when they occur, but the effect of the cycle is to cause a fatalistic attitude that the swings backwards and forwards are part of the natural order and cannot be broken.[2]

My own experiences in both the Quebec junior-college (CEGEP) system and at Athabasca University reinforce the perception that the regular and natural tendency to reorganize and to reallocate power and authority between central and regional entities often fails to achieve its real objectives (such as economies of scale, local responsiveness and better levels of service). Whether acknowledged or not, its primary function usually has far more to do with internal power politics than it does with direct benefits to the organization.

The regional 'model' at Athabasca, for example, has been altered four or five times in the past ten years, although most of the changes have been transparent to the student. They have principally involved reporting procedures (should there be a separate tutorial services unit, for example, and should it report to the faculties, to a separate director of regional and tutorial services, or to a vice-president?).

Every time regional reorganization is contemplated, it is contentious and takes on a high profile within the institution. This should not be surprising in a case where the local office offers a broad range of services because it thus raises power and control issues which affect most of the departments in the university. At Athabasca, for example, changes in jurisdiction or reporting procedures may affect the managers of the following departments whose services are offered directly via regional offices – registrar, finance, computing, faculties, tutorial services, course materials, plant and facilities, and public relations.

The primary issue of contention within the institution is power and control. To be effective, a regional office must offer coordinated and responsive services to the local community. It should take on its own identity, one that closely mirrors and responds to the local constituency. It follows that the local manager requires considerable power and autonomy over the range of services offered if this is to be achieved.

On the other hand, there are strong and legitimate requirements for central and professional control over such issues as academic standards (faculties), university regulations (registrar) and the costs of various services (all managers). In other words, there is a good case for both central and local authority, and the challenge is to get the mixture right. This is difficult enough in itself, but it is complicated by the natural tendency for both regional and central managers to control all aspects of operations within their purview and to protect their own interests in all cross-unit conflicts. While much interunit conflict can be avoided by spelling out jurisdictions and policies clearly and in writing, there will always be exceptions and grey areas not covered by previous experience which will require compromise or the seemingly inevitable involvement of top management.

That an effective regional organization is difficult to achieve should not be surprising. In the community-college system, the management of the direction and coordination of branch campuses in large institutions in Quebec and Ontario faces all of the same issues, and they are just as contentious and frustrating. Should each campus be given a large degree of autonomy under a powerful director or should their respective services be organized and directed by a team of central managers? Whether the answer is strong centralized control, highly autonomous satellites or a mishmash of compromises and committees, the problems of coordination and control persist, and attention soon focuses on the need for reform (echoing Brooke's earlier cited observation about the seeming inevitability of more tinkering).

This dilemma is not limited to educational institutions, but is a phenomenon common to all organizations where local agencies are dispensing services coordinated from a centralized core (as opposed to franchising or other forms of organization where the prevailing model is clearly a decentralized one).

DIFFERING REGIONAL AND CENTRAL VIEWPOINTS

The problems are best approached by examining them from the perspective of the regional and central managers, respectively. Unless the regional office is so large as to accommodate a number of staff in each of the service areas, it is usually the case that a few people represent the entire range of services to the general public. Hence, for our example, let's assume a regional office several hundred miles from the central facility, offering the following range of services to students – information, orientation, registration, admissions, course-materials pick-up, academic advising and counselling, seminars and classes, examination invigilation, computer labs, and library catalogue and circulation services.

The regional perspective. From the perspective of the regional office manager, it is critical that he or she have full authority for this range of services. As far as students are concerned, the regional office *is* the university, and they do not want to hear that the course materials are not available because of a foul-up in the central facility, or that the office staff do not have the authority to amend or break a rule or procedure in the student's interest – students just want the problem resolved, and they want it resolved immediately. If they are dissatisfied, it is the local staff and the local manager who will bear the brunt of the complaining, not the central-department staff who have almost no face-to-face contact with the student-customers, although they may have regular interaction by correspondence and telephone.

Physical distance adds to the problem. If local staff have no ability to interpret and apply policy to the specific case immediately before them, the quality of service to students usually suffers as the local staff try to contact central authorities for permission or decision. Even if the individual is immediately available or if systems have been established to cope with such requirements (such as a hot-line or establishment of regional concerns as priority issues), cases requiring a central ruling may be complex and contentious, and they may require the concurrence of more than one manager. This is more difficult to achieve without the personal presence of the key players. Although teleconferencing and other technologies can facilitate the process, central staff are less apt to be as responsive to inquiries from several hundred miles away as they would be under a system which resulted in their having to deal with someone standing in their own offices.

Another concern for the local regional manager is that such offices typically have a small number of staff, and it is imperative that each is flexible enough to do a wide variety of roles on a given day, especially when someone is absent because of illness or holiday. The manager is thus less concerned about specialized professional expertise and more concerned to hire staff who are flexible, adaptable and strongly service-orientated. This requirement for flexibility sometimes conflicts with central personnel policies and collective agreements, adding further stress to local office management.

The central perspective. From the perspective of a senior manager in the central facility, there are considerable concerns about quality and control of the given service. For example, the course-materials manager may be very concerned about the way the regions are handling distribution of materials, or the registrar might be more than a little concerned about reports that regional staff are bending the rules and regulations of the university, purportedly to provide better service to their local clientele. All central managers may be concerned about the lack of resident expertise within the regions to deal with major issues, particularly in professional areas where local staff training may be sufficient to guarantee the quality of service desired. This concern is exacerbated when regional offices are small and staffed primarily by clerical and administrative staff who may lack the education or training appropriate to dealing with the matter at hand. The larger central offices are more apt to have specialists with detailed knowledge and experience of their particular areas of responsibility which cannot be matched by more generalist staff in small regional offices.

There are also issues of the equitable distribution of resources and consistency in the application of policies. While a particular quality or method of service may seem absolutely necessary on a local level by a regional manager, the central manager of that service has a broader view of it across the institution and may have a legitimate concern that the university not offer wildly disparate levels of services in different communities. This has resource implications as well, so that a manager of computing services or plant and facilities may be opposed to a regional office's acquisition of computers or office furniture which costs more than is available to another office.

As has already been seen in Chapter 2, equitability (under the rubric of 'impersonality') is a principle central to a bureaucratic organization. Particularly in a university, where the 'core business' is handled almost exclusively by academic professionals, the underlying tension between equitability of service and a strong individual client orientation permeates the institution and is a major challenge for institutional managers.

POLITICAL AND VALUE-DRIVEN APPROACHES TO THREE CASE STUDIES

Thus, disputes tend to represent more than the usual conflicts over juris-dictions and authority, and it is because both the regional and central managers' concerns are legitimate that this is such a difficult area to administer. In pursuing the best way to manage regional networks, it is useful to look first at three typical issues of potential conflict between central and regional offices and to explore various responses to them, using Badaracco and Ellsworth's styles of leadership as guides. In each case, our sample student, the redoubtable Joe Trennis, is making a forceful request of his regional office counsellor, and the questions are what response is appropriate and who should make it in each case.

Case 1: Prerequisites. Joe needs one more course to graduate and wants to take an industrial psychology course which he feels very appropriate to his intention to take an MBA after his bachelor's degree. However, the psychology department has established Introductory Psychology as a prerequisite to these courses. While Joe has no formal credentials in psychology, he has read widely in the field and feels he already knows the material in the introductory course (which he has reviewed). If he is to graduate at the next convocation and hence not lose a year on his MBA, he doesn't have time to take both courses. The counsellor agrees with Joe's assessment of his knowledge and abilities and feels he would be wasting his time taking the introductory course. Should Joe be exempted from this requirement? Who should make the decision?

Case 2: Course materials. Joe is on a tight schedule and has now registered for his course. However, the university has a centralized course-materials inventory, and the counsellor informs Joe that he will have to wait for up to two weeks for his materials to be shipped to the regional office. Joe is upset because he had counted on working on the course immediately, especially because his job will take him out of the country next month, and he will have less time to focus on the course. The counsellor is sympathetic, having long lobbied for a regional distribution system so that students can benefit from 'one-stop shopping' and pick up their materials at the time of registration. This argument has recently been bolstered by a study from the university's institutional research department which has found a correlation between student success in completing courses and the speed of the university's response to his or her request for service. The manager of course materials has been resistant to this request because of the higher costs and administrative complexity of trying to manage several regional inventories. Should the university decentralize its course-materials distribution? Who should make the decision?

Case 3: Course suspension. Because Joe got a late start on the course, he is now concerned that he cannot finish its requirements within the designated six-month period. He would like to be able to suspend his study, without charge, for one month while he is away on business and to resume his studies upon his return – in other words, to be permitted to take seven months instead of six. The regional counsellor believes that this is a reasonable request, given that it was partly the university's fault in the first place for Joe's slow start, and given Joe's success in other courses. However, the registrar is the only official permitted to make exceptions to university regulations. Suspensions are not normally permitted because they tie up course tutors and thus deny places to other students. Given a long waiting list for the psychology course in question, and because institutional research has shown that the overwhelming majority of students who suspended study under a previous, more liberal policy, never actually completed the course, the registrar is apt to resist such an exception. Should Joe be granted a suspension? Who should make the decision?

It should be noted that a very similar case could be drawn up involving the conditions whereby a British Open University student is excused from attending its obligatory summer school.

RESPONSE 1: THE POLITICAL APPROACH

As Baldridge[3] has documented, such decisions are frequently made on a 'political' basis in universities. Hence, the decision will tend to follow the institutional power base, which is normally in the central offices and concentrated in the academic sectors (where, reason suggests, it should be in a university). It is likely that the cases would be handled as follows:

Case 1: Prequisites. Prerequisite courses are the exclusive domain of the appropriate faculty who are in the best position to know whether or not a given course requires specific prior knowledge. It is unlikely that Joe would receive permission to be exempted from the introductory course, and under no circumstances would the decision be made by anyone other than a faculty member, let alone a regional manager or counsellor.

Case 2: Course materials. The question of establishing a more decentralized distribution system for course materials would become a power (and a fiscal) issue in the institution, with the regional and central players vying for support among their colleagues. The regional manager would cite the institutional research and service to students as justification, while the course-materials manager would appeal to universal concerns about finances and build the central-system case on cost efficiency. The decision could go either way and would depend mainly on the credibility of the two key managers and on who lined up on either side of the issue. The 'political' leader would seek a compromise which would meet the major objections and objectives of both sides. Some probable outcomes would include a partial inventory of the most popular courses in local offices, or a very much more responsive and speedy distribution service from the central office, perhaps directly to the student's home.

Case 3: Course suspension. A strong case may be advanced both for making reasonable exceptions on a local level and for upholding registrarial control over any exceptions to established university policy. Under a political style of leadership, the appropriate executive officer would uphold the registrar's authority but urge considerably more responsiveness to regional and student concerns. A framework would be developed to encourage a close working relationship between the registrar and regional offices, within which it would be up to each regional counsellor to develop the best possible relationship with the registrar and to tailor arguments to his or her way of looking at things. This would probably mean fewer exceptions than the counsellor would make, and it would be very important to the registrar for it to be made clear that it was his or her decision in any case. A key factor in the registrar's decision would be the amount of pressure emanating from the faculties, especially if waiting-list students were putting a lot of pressure on them to provide course places.

RESPONSE 2: A VALUE-DRIVEN APPROACH

Things might look a little different under a 'value-driven' model of leadership. In the extreme case, if the single value of 'quality of service to students' was pre-eminent, the responses would be quite different, with the local counsellor or manager being given broad authority to make exceptions. The anticipated outcomes would be that the counsellor would be able to waive the prerequisite for Joe Trennis and approve a one-month suspension, and that the regional office would be able to hand out all course materials at the time of registration. Despite promoting themselves as student-orientated institutions, very few open universities would go this far, at least in part because of the difficulties of managing such a decentralized system.

More commonly, there would be at least two major values at the top of the university's priority list – quality of service to students (immediate decisions and services, no 'run around' in trying to find the appropriate authority) and the maintenance of the quality and integrity of its academic programme (decisions consistent with academic policy across regions). Consideration of this situation is a little more complex.

Case 1: Prerequisites. The decision about prerequisites would still be made by the appropriate faculty member or dean, but under somewhat different conditions. Given its strong commitment to service to students, the university would want to minimize the number of prerequisite courses and to ensure that a decision to establish a prerequisite was based on overwhelming evidence that students could not otherwise handle a particular course. It is likely that every prerequisite decision would have to be ratified by the senate or academic council and that a process would be established whereby a counsellor could get an immediate response from the faculty on a particular case (within a pre-established process and set of criteria permitting the counsellor to make such a request).

Case 2: Course materials. The governing value would be the quality of service to students, given that the location of the service would not be a factor in academic integrity. Hence, the manager of course materials would be instructed to find the most cost-effective way (such as through 'just-in-time' inventory systems, for example) to provide a full inventory to each of the regional offices. Hence, in most cases, students would be able to pick up their materials at the time of registration.

Case 3: Course suspension. This situation brings into conflict the two most important values of the institution. Unlike the political response, however, in this case, both the regional manager and the registrar would be put under strong pressure by the executive officer in charge to find a way through the two sets of values. Hence, rather than compromise or have a stand-off resolved (probably in the registrar's favour in the political scenario), the two managers would be expected to develop a cooperative system which takes the student's best interests into account within existing university regulations. The expected outcome would be a process whereby the on-the-spot counsellor would have authority to make exceptions under very specific conditions and/or a quick-response, hot-line service which would allow the counsellor to take cases not anticipated by prior policy to the registrar and get an immediate response so that there is no unnecessary waiting on the student's part. The point would not be so much 'who' made the decision as that every effort was being made to accommodate the student without violating the integrity of the university's policies. The latter would be monitored regularly and changed if necessary to satisfy these two objectives. The registrar's focus would shift from ruling on individual cases to ensuring that counsellors are knowledgeable about university policy and the rationale behind it, and to monitoring the application of policy through close liaison with regional offices.

ESTABLISHING REGIONAL OFFICES

The above analysis assumes conflict, ambiguity and competition between central and regional offices and looks at alternative ways of dealing with the resulting problems from several leadership perspectives. Regardless of style, however, the number, complexity and intensity of conflicts and problems can be reduced by the way in which regional networks are established in the first place. The following steps constitute a reasonable starting point in this direction:

• Jurisdictions and responsibilities must be very clearly defined between central and regional authorities, and reviewed regularly by both parties on the basis of their effectiveness in carrying out established policies and procedures.

- Regional staff must be subject to overall policy and it should be clear where and when they have to get official permission to deviate from it in the interests of a client.
- Within the reasonable limitations of the centralization – vs – decentralization dilemma, regional staff must have some leeway to respond to local needs without having to get central permission for every deviation from strict policy. If regional staff have to contact headquarters for every small decision, they become mere surrogate students. The students are not much better off than they would be making their own inquiries of headquarters, and the whole rationale for a regional office is undermined. At the same time, there are fundamental standards and principles of fairness which must be upheld, and it is not unreasonable to require official permission from central authorities if these are to be upheld. In an effective regional model, these fundamental standards are clear and understood by all, and there is considerable leeway on the details to allow local staff to give personal and prompt service.
- It is easier to say 'no' to a student by post or over the telephone. It is much more difficult to deny a student's request when he or she is ensconced in one's office and won't leave until it is granted. This goes beyond the notion that staff are more apt to bend rules in the physical presence of the student in that it recognizes that face-to-face encounters are more apt to result in the staff member's really listening and trying to understand the student's perspective than they are when reading a letter or talking on the phone. Staff are also more apt to question the university's policies and procedures if their interaction with students is more personal and intense, and hence regional staff have an important perspective on institutional policy which should not be ignored. The value of this direct feedback function of regional offices should be officially recognized and encouraged by the institution. At the same time, if regional staff understand central policies well, they may be better able to explain and get students to accept them because of the face-to-face relationship.
- Following from the previous point, an institutional value which encourages criticism and complaints from students is vital to any commitment to quality of service to students. It is not enough to provide for this through regional offices; systems must be put in place which ensure that complaints reach the appropriate authorities and that they are dealt with. This is particularly critical in open learning, given the already mentioned tendency for adult students to blame themselves rather than the institution when things go wrong (see discussion on pp 85–6 of Chapter 6). For many students, the most

frustrating aspect of dealing with educational institutions is not that something goes wrong (it always will) but that the institution is unresponsive when it does, or that no one seems to know who is the appropriate authority in a given instance.

- No set of rules and regulations can ever cover every eventuality. There are two extremes of response which are both unacceptable – the 'virtuoso bureaucrat'[4] who rigidly applies every rule in every case without exception, often to the point of stupidity (as when a clerk refuses to hand over course materials to a student because the latter forgot to bring the pink form that the clerk knows he or she has), and the employee who is incapable (or unwilling) to stand up to the student over the counter and bends the rules at will, with the consequence that students are treated unevenly and unfairly. It is important for the institution to recognize this and develop appropriate styles and skills in its front-line staff – those who deal directly with students on a regular basis.

- An additional component of central/regional differences is a function of what is usually a considerable dichotomy in their respective sizes. Large central offices evolve to deal with all of the problems faced by the institution, while regional offices are usually much smaller, staffed to the minimum required to offer all of the services. Consequently, there is a tendency for central offices to develop specialists and for regional staff to become generalists used to performing almost every function handled by their office. This specialist/generalist dichotomy further contributes to differing perspectives and misunderstandings between central and regional staff.

- A crucial response to the central/regional dilemma lies in staff development and training. Regional staff must understand why the rules are there, which ones are most important and how much leeway they have in applying them. Central staff need to develop a sensitivity to the sorts of concerns and pressures faced by regional staff and to be as adaptive and responsive as they can within the usual resource constraints. These objectives can be achieved in several ways:
  - internal exchanges, whereby regional staff work in the central offices and central staff in the regions. Hickman and Silva[5] quote the old adage, 'Don't judge a man until you've walked a mile in his shoes' to emphasize the value of such exchanges in sensitizing staff to each other's problems, concerns and perspectives;
  - promotion of central staff to regions and vice-versa;
  - staff development – this includes joint training sessions involving both regional and central staff, trainers from headquarters conducting workshops in regions (and vice versa), and regional staff visiting the central offices for orientation and discussion of common problems.

Some will object to these ideas on the grounds that they are too expensive, especially in terms of travel. I believe that this is one of the biggest mistakes typically made by an organization – when times get tough, the first budgets to be cut are the 'softer' ones like staff development and training. Given that any university's biggest investment by far is its existing staff, most of whom are tenured and will be around for some time to come, it follows that the continuing development of their skills and outlooks is critical to the success of the organization, and thus that this is one of the very last things that should be cut in tough times. This issue is taken up again in Chapter 10.

One additional concern common to most institutions with extensive regional operations is the challenge of implementing institutional change in such a decentralized system. This is especially difficult in institutions which are evolving quickly, where new policies, programmes and procedures are constantly being introduced, and where student enrolments and regional operations are growing quickly.

All of these factors characterize most new open universities as they grow in popularity and try to respond to more and more educational and social needs in their respective milieux. Special efforts will be required to ensure that regional as well as central staff understand the reasons for new staff and student policies, new fees, tighter fiscal controls, and changes in computer and other support systems. If institutional leaders do not make the effort to communicate personally with regional office staff, apparently successful institutional changes may be undermined by well-meaning but poorly informed staff in the regions who find it difficult to adjust to changes they do not understand in the first place.

It is not just regional offices which pose these difficulties, for there are many similar difficulties in the common practice of employing part-time, off-campus telephone and seminar tutors, the subject of the next section of this chapter on managing at a distance.

Managing off-campus tutors: dilemmas and contradictions

A second complex and contentious issue in a university dedicated to distance education is the management of off-campus tutors. While models vary from institution to institution, such staff are typically part-time, may live miles from the nearest campus or regional office, and are involved in any number of course-delivery activities, including telephone tutoring, classroom or teleconferencing seminars, classroom teaching at remote sites, and computer conferencing from home.

Given British organizational theorist Charles Handy's prognostication that organizations will increasingly hire staff part-time, and that a significant proportion of these will be working from their own homes,[6] the experience of open universities with part-time off-campus tutors is of interest well beyond the bounds of distance education.

THE ISOLATION OF OFF-CAMPUS STAFF

The following factors are central to the difficulties faced in managing such tutors:

- They are part-time, and their full-time commitment may be to another institution;
- They are usually on short-term or annual contracts, and their overall commitment to the institution may not be as strong as that of full-time permanent staff, especially if they have another full-time job;
- They do not have regular face-to-face contact with either their colleagues or their superiors, but tend to work in isolation from their homes;
- Their roles are frequently diffuse and not very well defined. As front-line staff, they usually represent the students' closest contact with the institution, but they lack the usual authority of the academic in the classroom because they are bound by courses designed by other staff and under the jurisdiction of a central academic. They may not even have any say in the design or content of the course, or in the marking of papers and examinations.

MANAGING AT A DISTANCE: TWO CASE STUDIES

Again, it would be useful to explore mini-case studies in confronting the problems of managing tutors at-a-distance. Our representative tutor in this case is Janet Trennis, a distant relative of the already mentioned Joe.

Case 1: Control of knowledge. Janet has been asked to return for her second consecutive year as on-site tutor for a sociology course offered in a remote northern community.

In this intensive course, 'tutoring' means 'teaching', in that Janet must reside in the community and meet the students every day. Given that most of her students are Native Canadians, many of whom are unmarried mothers, Janet feels strongly that an important component of her role is to adapt the course materials (examples, case studies) to the local environment and to the situations faced by single parents in today's society. However, she was frustrated last year when the academic in charge of the course refused to change the examination to reflect the supplementary materials she had introduced, and several of her students were very upset because they had failed the course even though getting good marks on the term papers (because the centrally set and marked final examination reflected neither the content nor the style of their local instructor). Hence, before accepting the course again this year, Janet has demanded that she alone be the marker for all papers and exams in the course, and that she be permitted to set the final examination. The course coordinator is very concerned about the implications of this for the course design, and especially for the overall standards, suspecting that Janet is 'soft' on the Native Canadian students and will mark them too easily. Should Janet's demands be granted? Who should make the decision?

Case 2: Breaking the rules. Janet is in trouble with her course co-ordinator. She has frequently in the past broken university rules in order to accommodate her students and, most recently, has given a student permission to take his examination three weeks after his deadline without consulting the course coordinator or registrar. Under university policy, only the latter has the authority to grant a course extension, and there is a small charge for the administrative inconvenience as well. Janet is unrepentant, although she admits that she should have consulted higher authority first. The student in question had been ill for some time and could not finish the course in time. However, in negotiation with Janet, he agreed that he could complete the course with a three-week extension. His past academic performance has been very good. Should the student be granted the extension? What should be done about Janet?

RESPONSE 1: THE POLITICAL APPROACH

Case 1: Control of knowledge. With most of the power vested in the faculties, it is highly unlikely that a political approach to this question would yield anything other than a reaffirmation of the status quo. That is, the concern for academic credibility would uphold the faculty's juris-diction over course design, course delivery and student evaluation. If Janet were to be given any leeway at all, it would be with the permission of the course coordinator. Janet's best approach, then, would be to lobby him or her or the dean, and perhaps to work with other tutors to convince the academic vice-president and, ultimately, the senate of the wisdom of making better provision for students with special needs. The same arguments could apply to students in penitentiaries, in companies or other specialized groups.

Case 2: Breaking the rules. Given that a university spokesperson, the tutor, had already told the student that he had the extension, the registrar or course coordinator would have no choice but to uphold the decision. The coordinator or dean would tread very warily before taking any formal action against Janet, fearing that the case could become a *cause célèbre* in the institution. He or she would carefully test the waters first to see which argument, service to existing students or maintaining places for those on the waiting lists, would gain the most political support. The issue would probably be resolved by giving informal support to Janet's concerns but asking her to 'go through the proper channels' in the future rather than making such decisions herself. Whether or not it subsequently became an issue would depend mainly on Janet – she might be content with this solution if it 'worked' for her in the next few cases. On the other hand, she might want to raise the issue more broadly in the institution, soliciting the support of tutors and faculty for more flexible services. In this case, it would become a major issue of values priorities in the institution and would ultimately be resolved by the responsible executive officer and/or the senate or academic council through policy change.

RESPONSE 2: THE VALUE-DRIVEN APPROACH

Case 1: Control of knowledge. Control of knowledge lies at the heart of an institution's educational philosophy. There are strong arguments for supporting Janet's position. No matter how well designed, no single set of course materials will be ideally suited to all student groups, and the ability to adapt materials and to bring them closer to the students' own experience is presumably one of the reasons for engaging a locally based tutor in the first place. It also follows that final examinations should reflect the actual course and that it is unfair to students if a major segment of what was discussed in class is not examined, or if they are examined on materials never covered. On the other side of the ledger, there are legitimate concerns about control of academic standards, about universal criteria and standards of student evaluation, and about the integrity of a course credit across all students. Under a value-driven leader, the issue would be taken well beyond Janet's particular case and addressed at the highest policy level in the institution first. Since both service to the student and overall academic credibility are fundamental values in the institution, it is to be expected that some changes will be made, but not at the expense of the central control mechanisms already in place. Possible responses would be:

- Permitting the tutor to set and mark a certain portion of the final examination;
- Much broader participation of tutors in the setting and marking of all examinations and in the design of courses;

- Special provisions for on-site tutoring for specific 'special needs' groups;
- An overall policy change which permits a 'local' component for all courses with the permission of the dean or vice-president academic.

Case 2: Breaking the rules. The decision in the particular case would be upheld for the same reason as stated for case one. A value-driven approach which placed the highest priority on service to students and academic credibility would be much more supportive of Janet's position than would a more political response. Within specified bounds, governed primarily by fiscal factors, tutors would be given a lot more leeway to treat students personally and individually, the emphasis being on the processes required to ensure that those affected by such decisions, notably the registrar, were kept informed about them. There would also be recognition within the institution that no rules or policies can cover all instances, and tutors might even be encouraged to bend the rules, provided they were fully aware of the consequences of their actions, and that they were operating within the specified limitations. The latter would be clearly determined by the fundamental values underpinning the institution's mission statement, and properly orientated tutors would not usually challenge them.

This approach would undoubtedly cause more problems for the central bureaucracy, but it would maintain the appropriate emphasis on the institution's espoused values of service to students and academic credibility rather than on administrative convenience. It would have to be monitored carefully, however, to ensure that one critical value, responsiveness to student needs, was balanced by another, equitable treatment of all, the professional–bureaucratic conflict which has formed the theoretical basis for this approach to university management.

Cost implications of regional networks and tutors

It would be misleading to suggest that all of the above issues are simply philosophical ones which can be resolved by reasonable debate among reasonable people. This is to ignore the cost of such services.

There is a presumption, not always proven, that the more services one offers, the greater the chances of student success. Hence, in addition to a basic home-study (correspondence) package, the university can offer all sorts of support – telephone tutors, teleconferencing, in-class seminars and lectures, library services, cassettes and videotapes, telephone and in-person counselling and advising, study-skills workshops, and others. Taken to an extreme, one alternative to distance education is to fly every student into posh facilities in a city centre, and another is to install a facsimile machine and personal computer in every student's home. These are interesting measures of the upper limit of an institution's costs per student.

Measures of cost effectiveness are essential to any decision-making in this area. For example, if 'course completion' or 'graduation rate' are the measures of success, the logical indices are 'cost per completion' or 'cost per graduate'. It is critical that institutions develop strong institutional research components, and that all policies about levels of service are constantly monitored and evaluated in terms of both cost and effectiveness. This is usually easier said than done, as it is notoriously difficult to isolate the variables and to standardize the timelines, especially if students are on individual timetables and have a lot of flexibility about when they finish courses and programmes.

This issue is examined in more depth in Chapter 6 in the discussion about developing learner independence.

Summary: combating institutional hypocrisy

The above case studies from two contentious areas, the management of regional networks and off-campus tutors, force the reader to challenge the basic value-systems which drive an open-learning institution.

Judging from its mission statements, its promotional information, and the speeches of its senior administrators, no educational institution has values higher than its academic integrity and a strong student orientation. In practice, every institution should be judged by the way it carries out these pious intentions. Does decision-making reflect the stated central values or are they too frequently undermined by power politics and administrative convenience?

Before elaborating on this point, I should make it clear that rules, procedures and systems are essential to the good management of any complex process. Administrative convenience is important if it results in better and more consistent overall service to all students. If every single case were considered in depth by every staff member, service to students would be slow and probably inconsistent, and therefore it would be unfair to some. So the point is not to abolish systems, rules and procedures, but to ensure that every rule and procedure has an important purpose, that the rationale for each is well and widely understood, and that there are clear and simple mechanisms for exceptions and appeals.

It is naive to think that organizational politics and convenience will not play central roles in decision-making, but these natural tendencies should be modified by the central values which are purported to drive the institution. No one knows better than its immediate clients, the students, how much institutional practice reflects these values, and hence they should be consulted and listened to on an ongoing basis (through such mechanisms as students' associations; student representation on various bodies; open seminars for staff which feature student panelists; focus groups with past and current students, both successful and unsuccessful; and mechanisms for exceptions and complaints which are effective and well understood by students and staff alike).

Even these measures can appear to be tokenism, however, especially in an institution where students are scattered over wide geographic areas and working at their own pace. It becomes very difficult to generalize about student needs or to find people willing to serve as student representatives, especially given expectations that they will truly represent others whom they do not know or have much capacity to consult. This means that open-learning institutions need to do even more than other educational agencies to ensure that staff know, support and demonstrate the central values on a daily basis.

Given the mini-case studies offered in this chapter, it is likely that decision-making in most open-learning institutions most of the time will resemble the political approach more than the value-driven one. The challenge is to not to eschew organizational politics and overtly wear one's heart on one's sleeve, but to provide leadership that will gradually reduce the gap between the two approaches; between the institution's promises and its actions. Before very long, the students will know the difference and, in the long run, so will everyone else connected with the institution.

Notes

1. Brooke, M Z (1984), *Centralization and Autonomy: A Study in Organizational Behaviour,* London: Holt, Rinehart & Winston, p 4.
2. Ibid, pp 3–4.
3. Baldridge, J V (1971), *Power and Conflict in the University: Research in the Sociology of Complex Organizations,* New York: John Wiley and Sons.
4. Merton, R K (1952), 'Bureaucratic Structure and Personality' in R K Merton, et al, *Reader in Bureaucracy,* Glencoe: Free Press, pp 361–71.
5. Hickman, C R and Silva, M A (1984), *Creating Excellence: Managing Corporate Culture, Strategy and Change in the New Age,* New York: New American Library, p 128.
6. Handy, C (1989), *The Age of Unreason,* London: Business Books, pp 79–87.

CHAPTER 8

Technology's the Answer – but What is the Question?

In distance education, it is so very rare
That you ever see a student (I wonder if they're there?);
From Canada to Tasmania, they're so very far away,
But there's one great magic answer that's always on display.

CHORUS: Technology's the answer,
    It gives you good vibrations;
    You never have to worry about humanistic relations.
    Technology's the answer,
    It's the latest thing today;
    Technology's the answer when you're far away.

Face-to-face interaction makes students seem uptight;
Sit them all at home instead and transmit by satellite.
And if the students pressure you in their search for the Holy Grail,
You can slow the whole thing down, using the Royal Mail.

CHORUS

There's no worry about discipline or students talking back;
A little bit of computerese will absorb any flak.
So if you're short of tutors and student-record clerks,
Just put it all on Telidon and let the machines do all the work.

CHORUS[1]

Chapter synopsis

New information technologies lie at the heart of the development of open-learning and distance-education systems on a worldwide basis. The case for adapting new technologies to the development and delivery of educational materials is a strong one, but, in almost every milieu, the actual experience of implementation has been far less successful than expected.

Working from the premise that this is far more the result of management problems than technological ones, the author explores the major issues and challenges faced in managing and integrating new information technology, using examples and case studies from both the educational and corporate sectors. In particular, he focuses on the unintended consequences of technological innovation, and how these can be avoided or anticipated.

Of all the challenges facing the modern manager, the integration and management of new technology may be the greatest. Technology can offer tremendous opportunities for competitive advantage through cost savings and exciting innovations, or a nightmare of escalating needs and costs, and an institution out of control. A bold new investment in technology can vault an institution into a leadership position in its field, or the unintended consequences of such a decision can have serious implications not only for the institution's competitive position, but also for the way it is managed and operated. For these reasons, it is the central theme of this chapter that senior management, not just those responsible for information technology, must be directly involved in major planning and decision-making in this area.

There are many examples of successes and failures in this area. Otis Elevator's well-publicized, centrally coordinated electronic-service system has allowed it to maintain a strong leadership position in its market niche, while Digital and Xerox have developed similarly successful systems in their respective areas. The banking industry has been revolutionized by the personal-touch banking machines, and supermarket checkouts and inventory-control systems have been similarly affected by the introduction of pricing bar codes on all products.

On the other hand, Emery Worldwide lost its strong leadership position in the courier business, at least in part because of a bifurcation between its information technology and strategic directions. As a result, it quickly lagged behind more integrated and innovative companies like Federal Express and Puralator. When the electronic calculator rendered the slide rule obsolete, the world's leading manufacturer of slide rules saw its business disappear from under it by failing to recognize that it was in the calculation business rather than the slide-rule business.

Universities are no exception to this requirement to integrate information technology into all strategic planning and development in an organization. As institutions dedicated to the creation and dissemination of knowledge in a knowledge society, they are particularly dependent upon information technology, not only for research and development but also for the daily management of their various structures and processes. Open universities rank very high on the list of organizations where information technology is not just a technical function, but is highly integrated into almost all of the institution's activities . . . or, at least, it ought to be.

The difference between the descriptive and normative aspects of the statement in the last sentence represents a major challenge for the leaders of today's open-learning institutions. By and large, information technology has not been an integral part of planning and development, but has grown in a piecemeal, topsy-turvy fashion. It has only been in the last few years, when institutional leaders have realized how dependent they have become on systems and computers, when departmental managers have found that their operations are increasingly affected by computing services over which they have virtually no control, and when executives are faced with computer capital and operating costs escalating out of control, that much attention has been paid to information technology.

The case for information technology (IT)

Whatever its abuses, whatever the problems in implementation, and whatever its cost, there can be no question that for more and more organizations, technology *is* the answer. Among its most evident advantages are the following:

- increased productivity;
- increased efficiency;
- innovation and product leadership;
- better quality of service;
- better decision-making;
- better management and coordination;
- better staff development and training.

Almost everyone has an opinion about new technology and its impact on modern society. At one extreme, there is the excitement and vision of MIT's Media Lab,[2] where the future seems very close as exciting innovations such as a personal electronic newspaper and cartoons that work out their own plots already exist in working prototypes. At the other, there is widespread concern, cynicism and alienation as a result of the Chernobyl disaster, the *Challenger* explosion and environmental pollution the world over, as thoroughly documented in James Bellini's *High Tech Holocaust*.[3]

The problems faced in managing and integrating new technology are not different in kind from those faced by all modern organizations, but they are particularly pertinent to open-learning institutions. For example, applying the list of advantages to the specific case of open-learning institutions might result in the sorts of considerations outlined in the following pages.

INCREASED PRODUCTIVITY

Course design and development. This is one area that stands to gain greatly from the advent of new technology, notably the tremendous capacity and flexibility of desktop publishing and the computer-graphics packages which accompany it. Cheaper and more portable systems which require less professional expertise can produce course materials far more quickly and cheaply than was previously the case.

The gains are not only financial. In the past, home-study packages have typically been left unchanged for at least five years because of the initial investment required to produce the materials. This has been associated by some writers with a reification of knowledge (Wolfe and Murgatroyd[4]) and a rigidity that is alien to the supposed flexibility of open-learning systems. With desktop publishing, however, course authors can modularize the materials and mail them out periodically to students. They can be revised regularly, and students can interact with them through electronic mail. This allows faculty to ensure that courses are up-to-date and adapted to the particular needs of a given learning group, modifications which were usually too time-consuming and expensive under the traditional 'print shop' technology.

Course materials inventory. The advent of a 'seamless' electronic production line not only benefits course production and revision, but it can also yield major benefits for the storage of course materials. Courses can be stored electronically rather than physically, and 'just-in-time' inventory systems can print out (or otherwise produce) course materials as required. This saves on storage space, and it means that there is no need to dispose of outdated materials or to close courses because unexpected demand has meant that materials have run out. Given the importance of course materials to distance-learning systems, this means changes in both the quality of materials and the responsiveness of services to students who await their course materials.

INCREASED EFFICIENCY

Admissions, registration and student records. Many open-learning institutions cater to the needs of individual students, permitting them to register at any time of year, to proceed through courses at their own pace, to take examinations at any time, and to extend or suspend studies if personal factors intervene. Each of these provisions is an admirable part of the institution's dedication to open learning, but it is often a nightmare to those responsible for designing and operating the support systems which make this flexibility possible.

Most universities and colleges have two or three registration periods in a year and can 'batch'-process student admissions and registrations. At many open universities, every student is on his or her own timetable, and batch-processing is not possible. Some students take more than ten years to complete a degree, and hence files must be kept 'active' much longer than is typical in a campus-based institution. The result of this flexibility is the need for far more sophisticated student-record systems, in terms of both design and capacity relative to the per capita student population. The advent of integrated computer systems has enabled institutions both to provide a faster and more responsive service to students and staff, and also to manage the whole area with fewer staff and less reliance on dull clerical work.

The management of student progress. Computerized tracking systems are essential when students are proceeding at their own rates. For example, Athabasca University has developed its own student-monitoring system which allows secretaries and faculty members to track the progress of each individual student. This also becomes an invaluable aid to course tutors, who are constantly having to make decisions about when to intervene with students who are falling behind or having difficulty with the course. Of course, if such systems are to be really effective, they must tie in to the central student-records systems as well, making a major demand on the system architecture . . . and added expense.

INNOVATION AND PRODUCT LEADERSHIP

Course delivery. There are widespread expectations that today's open university must be a world leader in the application of new technology to the delivery of education to remote students – through computer-assisted learning, computer-managed instruction, television, satellite networks, ISDN, interactive videodiscs, and facsimile machines, all to reduce 'turnaround time' and provide a more interactive environment for its students.

However pervasive these expectations, the record does not come anywhere near matching them. In fact, open universities are lagging behind even their traditional counterparts in the application of educational technology to the delivery of programmes and courses. Too much attention is often paid to the technology and not enough to the educational need. It is perhaps noteworthy that when the details of Athabasca University's new Canadian Distance-Learning Development Centre (CDLDC) were presented at a special event in connection with the international ICDE conference in Oslo, participants were overwhelmingly more interested in the 12 educational objectives set out in the strategic educational plan[5] than in the details of the technology.

Indeed, CDLDC offers an excellent case study of the difficulties faced in managing new technology. A consortium of the university, government agencies, and private companies in the computer and telecommunications businesses, it has been somewhat bogged down by disputes and misunderstandings about jurisdiction, goals and objectives, and management, even though its partners are unanimous in their commitment to its tremendous potential (this issue is pursued in Chapter 9 below).

BETTER QUALITY OF SERVICE

Any service institution which caters to a wide range of individualized services, and especially one serving widely dispersed customers, must place the highest premium on the quality of its services. This is central to the management of an open-learning institution, notably one employing distance-teaching methods.

Whether it is through reduced turnaround time via electronic student-records systems, computer-marked examinations, and computer-managed instruction; through more interaction among students and staff through two-way video and computer communications; or through better informed decision-making through up-to-date communications systems, the institution with up-to-date information technology is in the strongest competitive position to provide the best quality of service to students and other clients.

However, there is one strong proviso to this statement – given that the institution manages and integrates its technologies extremely well. This is explored in detail later in the chapter.

BETTER DECISION-MAKING

Quality of information. Maintaining a competitive edge in today's fast-changing society makes strong demands on a company's information systems. Chief executive officers and university presidents alike need sophisticated information systems to check their perceptions and visions against reality and to know what the competitors are doing. Long[6] notes that microcomputer systems are more conducive to this need than were centralized main-frame systems. While the latter may be very useful in marshalling data for a major decision, most executives gather information gradually and informally. Micro systems, which are relatively adaptable and accessible, are particularly well suited to the iterative decision-making processes followed by most executives. They also reduce the latter's dependencies on specialized analysts who may not understand exactly what the executive is seeking.

Institutional research. Institutional research, by definition, requires access to the institution's major information systems, including student records, student monitoring, financial information and human-resources systems. It is not enough to have good data bases, for an organization requires a high capacity to manipulate them through scenario building, hypothesis testing, and quality control. Objective data can often have a profound impact on decision-making, especially where they challenge or contradict 'institutional myths'.

At Athabasca, for instance, many staff ignored the problem of student dropouts when they thought the completion rates were over 50 per cent. When a 1981 study[7] revealed the actual rates to be less than 30 per cent, it precipitated an institution-wide preoccupation with this problem, and measures were taken which have gradually increased success rates to the level previously presumed. In another case, strong support for a very flexible, if expensive, course-suspension policy was quickly dissipated when a study demonstrated that fewer than 10 per cent of students who suspended their studies ever successfully completed the course.

BETTER MANAGEMENT AND COORDINATION

The management of regional offices. Especially at institutions like Athabasca University, where students can register daily and on-line in the regional offices, admission, registration and records systems must be particularly sophisticated. Regional clerks need access to files and policy in determining student eligibility for admission to or enrolment in a particular course. Not only does this put added pressure on system design, but it also raises important questions of security, access and jurisdiction. Many of the problems which are blamed on the systems and directed at managers of computing services are really the result of management decisions about who should have what decision-making power and information access. To the extent that these decisions are ambiguous or constantly changing, systems design and operation will be that much more complicated . . . and expensive.

Electronic mail. This is a very powerful management tool, not only for informing and consulting staff located in distant places but even within the same building. It is ideal for quick information dissemination or consultation on simple decisions. It has a big advantage over the telephone in that the manager does not interrupt the staff whom he or she is consulting, distracting them from whatever they were dealing with, and it avoids the common problem of 'telephone tag'. Instead, if staff are in the habit of checking their 'e-mail' frequently, they receive information quickly and when they are ready for it.

At the outset, some people feared that e-mail communications would be less personal and informal than telephoning or dropping in on each other. In fact, my own experience has been the opposite – it quickly becomes a very informal, friendly and often humourous mode of interaction, one that is efficient and effective in dealing with busy managers.

Computer conferencing. Electronic mail is well suited to short, snappy communications but bogs down if long documents are sent which require scrolling across many screens. Most managers react to this by running off a paper copy of the document, a practice which, at least in part, negates the whole value of e-mail in the first place.

Computer conferencing, whereby participants 'join' a particular topic and exchange viewpoints is better suited to broader, more philosophical issues and debates, but it is not as easy to adjust to as e-mail. Computer 'hacks', in particular, tend to love spending hours at the keyboard reacting to the opinions of their colleagues, but many others become frustrated with information overload and the amount of persiflage they have to scroll through. This process may improve in a number of ways – better systems which enable one to preview documents before having to read them (assisted by an effective conference 'manager'), and much better training in the use of this medium, given that many of us are still far more comfortable with the printed page.

BETTER STAFF DEVELOPMENT AND TRAINING

We are in the midst of a revolution in staff development and training as more and more companies recognize the essential need to continue to invest in their greatest resource – their existing staff. The Carnegie Foundation has estimated that corporate spending on education and training in America rivals the total annual expenditures of all American colleges and universities (in excess of $40 billion in the mid-1980s).[8]

Instructional-systems design and new technologies are central to what amounts to a revolution in corporate training, one in which distance-education techniques are playing an increasingly central role. A startling example is the teletraining concept developed by AT & T.[9]

Concerned about the high costs of training its huge sales and marketing network through conferences, seminars and other examples of face-to-face education, AT & T established a national teletraining network in 1981, which has grown to over 200 locations across the USA today, serving over 40,000 employees. The programme quickly achieved the projected cost savings of over 50 per cent, the high costs of travel and accommodation being avoided; it was less disruptive to the daily responsibilities of participants (another form of cost saving); but, more surprisingly, student acceptance of the teletraining was as high as for face-to-face instruction, learning levels were similar, and post-tests revealed those learning via teletraining to have a higher retention![10]

The Centre for Distance Learning at Athabasca University is capitalizing on this trend. The centre has already directed several successful externally-funded projects which combine instructional-systems design techniques and new information technologies to provide more effective and more cost-efficient training in both the private and public sectors.

There can be no question that the advent of new technologies is central not only to the development of distance education and open learning, but to all education and training in the 'knowledge' society. It is, however, one thing to recognize the potential and quite another to realize the benefits.

Major issues in information technology

Even if one accepts the tremendous potential for both qualitative and quantitative improvements offered by new technology, a number of crucial assumptions must be confronted and realized before the benefits will accrue. Discussion now turns to some of the pitfalls and challenges of managing change in this area, citing numerous examples from the world of open learning.

The above requirements converge to put tremendous pressure on systems development and management at an open-learning institution. This is discussed below within the context of the following:

- limits to computer capacity;
- priorities for systems development;
- unanticipated consequences and their implications for staff development;
- academic and administrative computing;
- centralized and decentralized systems.

LIMITS TO COMPUTER CAPACITY

In the author's experience, computer capacity is one of the few areas where supply drives demand. Typically, the manager of computing services is deluged by requests from other managers for new hardware, better software, quicker response time and more processing power. These demands exceed the current capacity by severalfold, so the manager cuts out the 'frill' requests, projects that the overall institutional capacity must double within five years, and submits a development plan which will satisfy the essential demands over that period. The surprising thing is that, if the budget process responds positively to this projection and allocates such major increases in the computing-services budget, within one year the manager's projections will be completely off, as represented on the graph (Fig. 8.1).

The reasons for this are not surprising. The increased capacity leads more managers to use the system and to develop their dependency on it, which often induces them to want to 'computerize' functions previously handled manually. This can result in a never-ending spiral of demand for computer capacity which regularly exceeds 'rationally' derived projections.

Another common aspect of this phenomenon is the tendency for institutions to bring in innovations (eg a new academic programme, more flexible academic regulations, new independent projects) without considering their technological implications. While academic decisions, such as a new degree programme, must drive all support systems in a university, they should not be made in ignorance of their implications for computer systems. Otherwise, costs will inevitably exceed all expectations.

Finally, all systems have 'bugs' in them which must be fixed, and the experience of operating systems on a daily basis will inevitably suggest ways in which existing systems can be improved. It is very difficult to resist the temptation to amend or enhance systems where there is apparently an immediate payoff, but the net result of many such decisions can dramatically alter the nature and real costs of a given system.

PRIORITIES FOR SYSTEMS DEVELOPMENT

Typically, requests for systems development (acquisition of hardware and software, networking, additional staffing) far exceed the institution's ability to respond to them. If, as is so often the case, priorities are set through an essentially political process, development may be haphazard, unbalanced and inconsistent with the other priorities of the institution.

A value-driven approach links priorities for systems development directly to overall institutional priorities, ensuring close integration

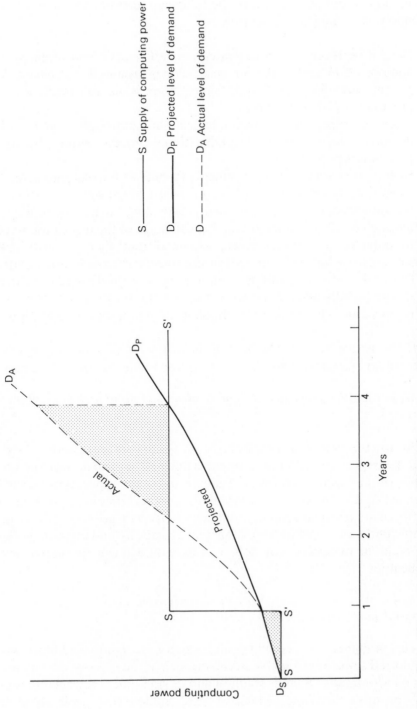

Figure 8.1   *This graph indicates how additional computer supply can influence demand*

between overall, long-range and strategic planning and planning for information technology. Moreover, any additional investment in technology should be subject to the following sorts of criteria as a vital component of the assessment process:

- Does it represent a demonstrated cost efficiency? Too often, such add-ons never realize the financial savings promised, but once new systems are developed, it is almost impossible to revert to the previous way of doing things.
- Does it represent a technological breakthrough which will demonstratively improve the educational process (within the cost parameters permitted)?
- Does it provide a direct improvement in service within cost parameters?
- Does it represent a quantum leap forward which will revolutionize the industry or give a clear competitive advantage to the institution?
- Does it contribute to the technological image of the institution so as to enhance its marketability, provided that there is also real substance to this perception? If the innovation is brought in primarily for window-dressing and promotion purposes, this limited objective should be fully understood so that no one has the illusion that it represents a more fundamental technological change for the institution.

If the above are the major criteria in favour of investing in new technology, managers should be wary of the following sorts of claims:

We just need this additional hardware/software and all our problems will be solved.

All too frequently, as noted above, projected costs are understated, and the impact of further investment is felt well beyond initial expenditures, or the staffing, operating, training and other implications of such capital acquisitions are underestimated. Another common mistake is to try to solve such management problems as uncertain priority-setting and inefficiently used staff by 'throwing' more hardware and software at the problem, an expensive and inefficient method that usually creates new difficulties.

I know it's a lot of money, but we've already spent a million. If we don't spend more, we will lose the value of the initial investment.

This argument is seductive and cannot be ignored, but it has supported some questionable decisions such as the colossal overspending on Montreal's Olympic stadium and its subsequent retractable roof or Toronto's Skydome, which at $512 million cost triple its 1985 estimate.[11] A useful tool for confronting this argument is an effective managerial accounting system which evaluates future benefits and costs rather than what has already been spent. On occasion, it does make sense to cut a project even though the initial investment has been heavy. Athabasca University made such a decision with Telidon, the Canadian videotext system, after several years of experimenting with its application to course development and delivery. Such decisions are difficult at the time, especially because they antagonize those who have developed strong vested interests in the project, but they should always be made in the context of the benefit of the future investment, rather than on the argument of what has already been spent (which can sometimes be a form of blackmail).

If we don't acquire this new technology immediately, we'll fall behind the competition.

While one cannot ignore the impact of technology on competitive position (as Baldwin and Harley-Davidson learned from Yamaha pianos and motorcycles, respectively), there are also dangers in being 'first in' with a new technology. The institution has to find an appropriate balance between being on the 'cutting edge' and ensuring that its investment is secure. An appropriate response here is to run carefully monitored pilot projects before adapting the entire organization to the innovation.

The industry is quickly moving to universal standards and product compatibility, so we don't have to worry too much about fitting the two systems together.

However encouraging are recent attempts to develop universal standards, trying to match incompatible systems can be time-consuming and expensive, and it sometimes just cannot be done. It is not always easy to get reliable advice here. IT managers may have strong brand loyalties (computer companies work hard to see that they do), and executive officers are susceptible to signing agreements with new dealers who offer 'irresistible' packages – from both tendencies have many bad decisions followed!

If we don't computerize this system, the whole place will fall apart.

A healthy scepticism is useful here. For example, it may sometimes be appropriate to stick with an effective paper system. Too often, the dependable old system looks very good in retrospect to a manager whose implementation of an electronic one has disrupted staff morale, cost more than projected and developed an unacceptable dependence on another unit's staff and machines.

A recent attempt by three of us to board a plane illustrates a misuse of technology. We asked the air hostess at the control desk to find three seats abreast (window, aisle, aisle) with no one stuck in a middle seat. Keeping an ever increasing line of passengers waiting, she spent about 10 minutes on the computer trying to come up with the right combination for our 50-minute flight. She finally succeeded, but only after an embarrassingly long wait in front of other passengers (we tried to withdraw the request after a few minutes but she insisted on continuing). When we got on board, the plane was about three-quarters empty, with at least 15 rows offering the desired seating pattern. One is quickly reminded of the time when airlines had diagrams of the plane interior and put small stickers on the seat numbers as people were assigned. This was fast and efficient and would have served us well on this occasion.

This new computer system will save us three staff positions over the next five years.

This is a favourite justification, which may be realized. However, unless the manager is required to pinpoint the exact positions and held to the savings once the new systems have been introduced, the savings are usually more hypothetical than real – 'Without the new system, we would have had to hire three more people this year'.

In each of these cases, it is incumbent upon senior managers to challenge assumptions and assertions in the same way that they would in any decision-making arena, instead of being intimidated by technological jargon or seduced by a glamorous new product.

UNANTICIPATED CONSEQUENCES AND THEIR IMPLICATIONS FOR
STAFF DEVELOPMENT AND TRAINING

All too frequently, innovations in technology have major impacts on the way an organization operates which were unanticipated or unintended at the time of their introduction. Among the most common are:

Impact on hierarchy. Long[12] cites Leduc's Bell Canada study which found that computer conferencing broke down the company's formal hierarchy, an impact that had not been anticipated when the system was introduced. He suggests that the impact of microprocessing is usually to produce smaller and flatter organizations with more evenly shared authority than was the case under more centralized macrosystems.[13]

Distribution of power. It follows from the preceding point that new technologies can have a direct impact on the distribution of power and authority in an organization. A particular problem here is a feeling, sometimes quite valid, of loss of control by a manager.

A classic case in the university setting involves a decision to computerize student-record systems. When paper record models are replaced by central student-record systems, a registrar may suddenly find himself or herself unduly dependent upon computing services for the day-to-day functioning and management of this service. If the systems 'go down', the registrar's office stops functioning; or, if computer response time is slow, service to students suffers. The real problems arise when the registrar feels that insufficient priority is being given to these concerns by the computing services unit. This requires intense lobbying, on behalf of the registrar, of the manager of computing, who, in turn, might be subject to similar arguments for more support from other user groups.

The net impact is a feeling of loss of power by managers who are being held accountable for services over which they no longer have full authority. One solution, that of giving user group managers more control over computer resources, has its own problems (as discussed on pp 137–9 below).

Managerial and secretarial roles. Word processing has led to an interesting change in what executives do. The convenience of the microcomputer has meant that many executives now do their thinking in front of a computer screen and are doing more and more of the 'typing' once performed by a secretary. The latter's traditional activities of typing and filing are no longer so onerous, and he or she is thus freed for other support activities, such as formatting, initiating standard response communications from computer files, or taking on higher-order or more personal tasks than previously.

Time-saving an illusion? The result is not always time-saving, however. Since word processing makes it so easy to edit a manuscript, there is a new tendency for executives to 'fiddle' with a letter, speech or report for far too long, making amendments which previously would have involved someone's retyping an entire document. It is not even certain that this produces better-written manuscripts, and it probably produces longer ones!

The dependency that word processing fosters can also be extremely frustrating when things go wrong. There are many ways to lose a file completely in a way that was not previously a problem, and virtually every computer user (and probably especially book authors!) has learned the hard way of the necessity of making frequent backups of all work. Another common difficulty, also encountered by me while

producing this manuscript, is the incompatibility of various systems
(even a standard software package such as Word Perfect has many
different versions according to the vendor, disc size and date), which
can be very frustrating when attempting to write in different locations,
print from different printers or supply the appropriate version to pub-
lishers or other users.

Employees working at home. One of the most interesting outcomes of
microprocessing is the potential for employees to work at home instead
of coming into the office each day. A few companies have actively
encouraged this, such as the Dutch newspaper cited by Long[14] which
pays some people 2000 guilders (£600) a month extra to work at home
(recognizing its own capital savings in not having to provide office space
for these workers). Distance education lends itself readily to this
practice. At Athabasca University, where almost all professional
employees have their own computer terminal and/or microcomputer,
more and more academics and editors are writing courses at home.

If, as Handy[15] suggests, this is to be the pattern of the future, it raises
a number of very interesting questions. While it is sometimes cited as
advantageous to employees, usually women, who can work at home and
look after their children at the same time, this brings back familiar
concerns about the exploitation of women trying to do two jobs at once,
especially if it also 'reisolates' them socially.[16]

Another issue about which very little has yet been written but which
is already in evidence at Athabasca are the implications for management of having so many professional staff working at home. Deans and
other managers are learning to communicate electronically rather than
in person and, while this may be effective in monitoring the work of individuals, it renders far more difficult the building of a strong academic
'climate' or social support group. In short, managers are having to learn
new ways to manage in environments where staff are connected electronically rather than in person.

Health hazards. While not completely documented, there is strong
evidence, in Canadian, British and American studies, that display
terminals are health hazards, especially to pregnant women.[17] They may
also tie employees to their desks in a new form of boring, repetitive
labour (often organized like the former typing pools). Despite some of
these concerns, there is room for optimism, however. Long reports that
the majority of studies of lower-level employees who have had to adapt
to microprocessing indicate that both their job satisfaction and productivity have increased, new opportunities have become available to them
and their response to the changes has usually been positive.[18]

How one introduces technological change is apparently as important as the nature of the change itself. In distance education, desktop publishing threatens jobs and procedures in established print shops; electronic mail and computer conferencing change management practices, and the computerization of information and systems can alter power balances and management styles throughout the institution. While lip service is usually paid to training staff to cope with technological change, this often falls far short of what is required:

- Attention quite naturally focuses on the positive attributes of the innovation, and potential problems are either overlooked or minimized.
- Change is often threatening, especially if it requires staff to rethink the way they do things or to develop new skills in areas where they have some apprehension. The psychological aspects of technological change are frequently underestimated.
- Senior managers may have to change the ways they make decisions, given the power of electronic information systems both in support of and as a challenge to their traditional power bases.
- While the decision-making process may be long and agonizing for top management, the time frame for implementation is often very swift once the decision is made. Hence, new systems and processes are sometimes brought in too quickly for proper attention to staff training.
- The brunt of systems changes is usually borne by support staff, who are disadvantaged in their capacity to adapt to change in comparison to professionals. They lack the educational background, the institutional overview, the freedom to organize their own time, and perhaps the broader organizational commitment which facilitate one's ability to cope with change.
- Sufficient time may not be taken to ensure that the trainers themselves fully understand the roles and perceptions of their clients.

All indicators point to the importance of a carefully thought-out plan of implementation which involves and is sensitive to the concerns of all employees affected. In a three-nation study of the impact of information technology on the workplace, Land reported that changes were most often successful when open and informal means were used to introduce them, whereas deskilling and alienation were more frequently the result of a 'deterministic, rationalistic' model of managerial behaviour.[19]

The message is clear. Technological change is inevitable, and it is often very desirable, but it can be dysfunctional unless those affected by it are involved in all aspects of its implementation, from the initial planning and decision-making to the details of its application in the workplace. By consulting the affected parties directly, senior management can ensure that staff understand the reasons for change and that their legitimate concerns are taken into account in implementation. Moreover, such a process of consultation may also have an impact on the ultimate decisions, given that front-line staff are seldom quite so enamoured of the latest technology as are their supervisors.

There is strong evidence that IT managers themselves have learned the lessons of earlier years. In a study of 28 senior British IT managers, Earl found that they ranked management and organizational issues as the key variables in their own success and that they ranked technological issues last![20] This has implications for the training needs of such managers, who are usually recruited to their positions primarily on the basis of their technological expertise.

ACADEMIC AND ADMINISTRATIVE COMPUTING

One of the most common organizational problems in a university is whether or not 'academic' computing services (support for research, course design and development, course delivery, student evaluation, computer-aided instruction and computer-managed learning) should be separate from or part of the overall computing-services division.

The preferred model is usually to separate them, recognizing that the academic issues, which tend to be longer-term and more free-wheeling than the bread-and-butter nature of such key administrative requirements as financial and student-record systems, might not otherwise be given the priority they deserve. It is thus clearer what the relative priorities are if there is an absolute distinction between the resources available to each and if they are managed separately. It should be noted that this sort of division does not always happen by design. In one case in a Montreal college, the decision to separate the two divisions was made when a vice-president found the respective managers rolling on the floor in an all-out physical battle over use of the centralized resources.

At the same time, separation of the two does not guarantee the absence of conflict. The academic computing division usually requires support and maintenance from the central computing services division, and both departments compete for resources at budget time. Again, central support for academic computing should be determined by overall institutional plans rather than the immediate priorities of the computing services department.

One approach to this, just being implemented at Athabasca University at the time of writing, is to distinguish between all service functions (computing services division) and research and development (academic computing division). While the distinction is somewhat artificial and difficult in the case of certain applied projects which may be both research and service at the same time, it is useful in encouraging the recruitment of researchers who will not be deflected from their primary tasks by constant requests for service and training, and in underlining the responsibility of the computing services department for all service and support.

Nevertheless, there are important distinctions between the institution's administrative services (registrar, financial and human resources systems) and services to academic computing. These are recognized in the AU model by the creation of an educational computing services unit within the central computing department, which is dedicated to the needs of academic users and located in the research-and-development unit of academic computing. Once defined for a given time period, human and other resources cannot be transferred between administrative and academic services support without the agreement of both vice-presidents responsible for the service and academic sides of the university, a reflection of the importance attached to senior-management control of IT processes.

Another feature of overall institutional control of priorities and the optimum use of resources is the creation of an educational users' advocacy group, which is responsible for establishing priorities for the academic sector so as both to direct and support the allocation of central computing resources to academic service and development priorities.

One should have no illusions about 'control' here. In fact, some of the problems are disappearing with the rapid advent of personal computers and workstations. As these become more powerful and less expensive, computing support for academic work will become increasingly a part of what academics bring to their roles, and less and less an institutional service requiring institutional management.

However, even as personal workstations replace faculty desks in the institution, new issues arise, such as control of the quality of production and linking individual workstations into central data and production systems, and chapters like this one will have to be rewritten almost annually to keep up with the managerial implications of new developments in technology.

CENTRALIZED AND DECENTRALIZED SYSTEMS

The debate over whether or not computing resources should be distributed and managed in a centralized or decentralized way is being obviated by the rapid development of microtechnology which enables departments to develop their own processing and networking capacities with less and less reliance on a central facility.

Just a few short years ago, economies of scale favoured centralization, but as hardware costs have come down and the lessons of the need for specialist–user interaction and responding to very diverse requests have been learned, Earl believes that the case for the centralization of information processing is a 'lost cause'.[21]

> The centralisation–decentralisation argument, as ever, was an exercise in seeking a balance between effectiveness and efficiency and in managing ambiguity. Now, with dispersing technologies, the balance has to be redrawn, the ambiguities are more complex and the IT managers have to reassess their demand and redeploy their resources.[22]

While microprocessing has many advantages, it also poses problems, especially for the distribution and security of data bases (such as student academic records, personnel and payroll data, and other financial information). The answer presumably lies in some combination of an integrated and secure central system with distributive capacity to smaller local systems, and it will be facilitated if and when the computer industry manages to develop common standards and protocols which allow for free-flowing communications among the various machines and users.

Another aspect of this issue is the question of who should have responsibility for the management of information technology. While the primary players are the institution's senior executive and the manager of its information technology department(s), some institutions have successfully devolved this to other line managers.

For example, given the registrar's responsibility to manage the student admissions, registration and records systems, a strong case can be made to have programmers and technicians assigned directly to the registrar's office rather than having the department dependent upon services from a computing services department. The advantage to the registrar's office is that it can be assured that its own developmental and maintenance priorities are addressed and that it can intervene directly if there are major problems with the systems. However, if this is carried too far, it causes a similar problem for the manager of the 'computing services department, who can no longer be held responsible for system maintenance and development because so many of the resources are under the control of other managers. This is not a necessary outcome, but it is inevitably the result of a failure to integrate information technology planning with strategic planning.

One solution is to designate officials like the registrar 'systems manager' for appropriate components of the institution's systems (eg admissions, registration and records). Computing staff remain within the computing services unit, but a specific personnel and computer-time component is dedicated to systems under the registrar's jurisdiction.

The latter is responsible for establishing priority areas and ensuring that the institution's (registrar's) needs are optimally addressed by the dedicated resources. While it still requires excellent cooperation between the registrar and the management of computing services, this model helps clarify roles, reduces ambiguity and overlaps, and allows both managers to pursue their responsibilities in tandem and in the best interests of the institution as a whole.

Conclusion: leadership responsibility of senior management

Following a 15-company study of line executives who had been proactive in information technology, information systems expert John Rockart concluded:

> If war is too important to leave to the generals, the deployment of infor-
> mation technology is far too important in 1988 to be left to information
> technologists.[23]

Rockart traces IT development through four phases – from the accounting era of the 1950s and early '60s, which was dominated by information systems; through the operational era of the '60s and '70s, which brought many of an organization's systems 'on line'; and the information era of the late '70s and early '80s, ushered in by improved 'fourth-generation' user languages, relational data bases and personal computers; to today's 'wired society', when line leadership in strategic systems has become essential.

This is a significant change for senior executives, and many are ill-prepared for it. The past decade has seen major frustrations in many organizations as generalist managers try to understand the technology and jargon of computer and systems development. The need for change applies not only to the generalist manager, but also to the informational technologists themselves. The latter can no longer hide behind their jargon and technology but must communicate as clearly as they can with their various clients within the organization. Priority setting can no longer be left to individual managers but must be integrated into the overall strategic planning of the institution. There is more than a little irony in the frequency of poor communications between departments devoted to management information systems and the rest of the institution.

This leads us back to our concern about leadership from the top. Senior executives, and particularly the chief executive officer (university president) must be assertive and doggedly persistent in challenging the cost and complexity of proposed developments in the IT area. It is only through a combination of a strongly integrated strategic-planning process, an information technology director who is a good communicator and teacher, and a chief executive officer who stays abreast of developments that an organization will have any chance at success in this complex and fast-changing arena.

Briefly, this translates into an institutional programme that looks something like the following:

Strategic planning. A strategic plan for the allocation of IT resources will be developed and approved by the senior management of the institution to ensure that their use best reflects institutional priorities.

Priory setting. An annual priority-setting process, approved by senior management, will identify what specific resources will be allocated to each of three aspects of systems development:

— *Maintenance.* Specific positions and resources will be identified for this function, and no others will be diverted to it. 'Maintenance' will be carefully defined to include crisis response and alterations to existing systems which are driven by the institution's priorities and IT strategic plan.

— *Prototypes.* Where new development is required, specific and limited resources will be identified for the development of prototypes which specify the system requirements and the alternative responses to them. These prototypes require close cooperation between the user department and the computing-services department, and some of the resources will be supplied by the former. No enhancement or development project should go forward unless it has gone through this stage, one outcome of which might be a decision that a computerized system may not be required.

— *Development.* Some resources will be reserved for this function, but no systems enhancements or additions will be considered until they have gone through the prototype stage.

This approach, or one very like it, which ensures senior-management control of the application of IT resources, is essential if the institution is to yield the expected benefits of system development. While some might advocate more control for the director of IT or computing services, this top-down approach actually provides more support to the latter position by making institutional priorities clear and shielding him or her from ongoing pleas for projects from other managers. The IT director's job is then to ensure that the promised developments and services are provided and that objectives are met by the dates specified. Depending on resources, some leeway can be provided for within categories, and the director may have some 'floating' resources to apply to unexpected situations, but it is very easy to lose control here if the overall process is not respected and adhered to in considerable detail.

Ultimately, unless the planning, priorities and management of information technologies mirror the organization's central values and directions, they will hinder rather than facilitate the attainment of the institution's mission and goals. The concern is not just for the management of new technology, but for a strategic response 'which reflects the fundamental nature of the changes faced as a result of new information technology'.[24]

Notes

1. Paul, R H, (1982), ICCE Musical Revue, Vancouver, BC, in Daniel, J S, Stroud, M R and Thompson, J A (eds), *Learning at a Distance: A World Perspective,* Athabasca University, p 307.
2. Brand, S (1988), *Media Lab: Inventing the Future at MIT,* New York: Penguin.
3. Bellini, J (1986), *High Tech Holocaust,* San Francisco: Sierra Club Books.
4. Wolfe, R and Murgatroyd, S (1979), 'The Open University and the Nego-tiation of Knowledge, *Higher Education Review*, 11: 2, pp 9–16.
5. Strategic Planning Group (1988), 'A Strategic Educational Plan for the Canadian Distance-Learning Development Centre', Athabasca University, April, section 3.
6. Long, R J (1984), 'The Application of Microelectronics to the Office: Organisational and Human Implications' in Piercy, N (ed), *The Management Implications of New Information Technology,* London: Croom Helm, p 103.
7. Shale, D (1982), 'Attrition, A Case Study' in Daniel, Stroud and Thompson, op cit, pp 113–17.
8. Eurich, N P (1985), *Corporate Classrooms: The Learning Business,* Princeton, N J: The Carnegie Foundation for the Advancement of Teaching, p ix.
9. Shute, A G et al (1986), 'Teletraining in the Corporate Environment', Cincinnati: Sales and Marketing Education Division, AT & T, 6 pp.
10. Ibid, p 3.
11. *The Globe and Mail,* 14 July, 1989, p A4.

12. Long, op cit, p 98.
13. Ibid, p 103.
14. Long, op cit, p 106.
15. Handy, C (1989), *The Age of Unreason,* London: Business Books, p 113.
16. Long, op cit, p 106.
17. Ibid, pp 110–11.
18. Long, op cit, p 113.
19. Land, F (1984), 'The Impact of Information Technology on the Workplace' in Piercy, N, *The Management Implications of New Information Technology,* London: Croom Helm, pp 75–94.
20. Earl, M (1984), 'Emerging Trends in Managing New Information Systems' in Piercy, N, *The Management Implications of New Information Technology,* London: Croom Helm, pp 197–8.
21. Earl, op cit, p 194.
22. Ibid.
23. Rockart, J F (1988), 'The Line Takes the Leadership – IS Management in a Wired Society', *Sloan Management Review* (Summer), p 59.
24. Piercy, N (1984), 'Management and New Information Technology' in Piercy, N (ed), *The Management Implications of New Information Technology,* London: Croom Helm, p 5.

CHAPTER 9

The Politics of Collaboration*

Chapter synopsis

Open-learning and distance-education institutions are ideally suited to collaboration with each other, and with both public- and private-sector institutions. In fact, this collaboration is often essential to their effectiveness, as they are often not, in themselves, the 'whole' answer to a student's requirements.

Building on examples from both the private and educational sectors, the author scrutinizes both successful and unsuccessful collaborative agreements and offers some rules and suggestions to govern whether or not a collaborative venture is a good idea in a particular case.

We live in a time of mergers, takeovers and networks as the world moves closer and closer to a global economy. The pace of change is astounding – the Eastern Bloc tentatively embracing capitalism, the 'chunnel' under construction between England and France, China opening up and closing again very quickly, and the rapid division of the world into major common-market and free-trade blocs.

The changes are no less dramatic on the education front. Gigantic new open universities have opened in the past 15 years in China, India, Thailand, Indonesia, and elsewhere as earlier extensions of educational opportunity now carry into the postsecondary sector. These institutions are less affluent than their Western counterparts (Athabasca University, the British Open University, the Open Learning Authority, La Télé-université, the Fernuniversität, the Dutch Open University) and in less of a position to invest so much in initial course development. This has led to requests for assistance, notably in the selling of courses between insti-

---

*The material for this section has been adapted from a paper presented by the author at a conference on 'Recent Trends in Adult Education in Canada and the United Kingdom', sponsored by the Centre for Canadian Studies at Queen's University, Belfast, in May 1989.[1]

tutions and in joint development of courses and course delivery systems.

Without denying the natural tendency of people in organizations to want to do things 'their' way, there is increasing realization that there are many benefits to cooperation and collaboration in the world of distance education and open learning.

The pressures for collaboration and networking come from both internal and external forces.

External pressures for collaboration

External pressure comes in the form of pressures from government to reduce taxpayer subsidization of higher education by encouraging universities to diversify their funding bases and to 'privatize' some of their functions. This trend is satirized unmercifully in a recent British book in response to the Thatcher government's preoccupation with the privatization of virtually everything, including water, Frank Parkin's *The Mind and Body Shop*.[2]

There is a strong push for system integration and rationalization, a tendency by government to see universities not as autonomous institutions but as the apex of a coherent and integrated educational system in which each level and each institution has its specific role, one which complements all the others, so that the best possible range and quality of educational provision is made to society. Although this perception is contrary to traditional notions of universities as independent organizations free from political interference, the relatively new reliance on public purses has seriously compromised university freedom to resist pressures for system integration.

Accessibility to higher education, following naturally from earlier pushes for the democratization of primary and secondary education, has become a surprisingly strong political issue, not only in developing countries but in the developed West. Hence, the conservative Social Credit government of British Columbia, the Progressive Conservative government of Alberta and the Conservative government of the United Kingdom have all placed a high priority on the provision of more places for university students, not least through their support of open-learning institutions. This has come, however, not so much in the form of increased grants as in incentives and requirements for close collaboration among the various institutions – colleges and universities in British Columbia's 'university college' model, colleges and universities under Alberta's 'capstone' concept, and 'open' learning institutions and industry throughout Britain via such agencies and schemes as Flexistudy, the Open College and the Open Tech.

More crassly, universities are encouraged to collaborate with each other and with other institutions in order to curry favour with the party in power. A major issue for universities these days is when to play along with and when to resist 'tied' government funding of specific initiatives. There is more than a suspicion of hypocrisy here when university presidents make stirring speeches decrying the threats to university autonomy posed by government intervention, and then fall over each other trying to win government contracts which are tied to very specific political and social policy. They complain a lot about the rules but are as eager as ever to play the game and win the prizes.

As in the business world, universities are being forced to collaborate because of the entry into postsecondary education and training of new agencies, including private corporations, and through increased competition among the universities themselves.

These pressures notwithstanding, there are a number of internally driven reasons why universities are pursuing more collaborative ventures with other institutions and agencies.

Internal pressures for collaboration

Cost efficiency – at least in theory, there are major cost savings to be gained by pooling resources with another institution. For example, Athabasca is the lead institution in the development and delivery of an entrepreneurship course in Canada's four western provinces and two northern territories (although the cost savings may be more illusionary than real, as discussed below). In Britain, a number of schemes, including the Open Tech programme, the first efforts of the Open College, and agreements between the Open University and the National Extension College to provide support services to each other have been driven, at least in part, by concerns for cost efficiency. The Indira Gandhi National Open University in India has formal agreements with many institutions, including Athabasca, the British Open University and the Open University of British Columbia, while the last-named is involved in several joint programme development projects with other institutions, including Australia's Deakin University.

More philosophically, there is a case for suggesting that the whole may be greater than the sum of its parts – the synergy that comes from collaboration can often yield benefits well beyond those originally envisioned. Of course, it follows that the reverse can happen as well, with the main by-product being headaches. Experience here closely parallels industry's experiences with mergers and takeovers – for every Unisys, widely regarded as a successful merger between Sperry and Burroughs, there are many more failures, giving rise to a wide range of literature analysing why they did or did not succeed. It is interesting to

– the ways in which the two institutions match or don't match on such issues as management style and communications.[3]

An excellent example of meeting new needs by forming organizational entities is the $7.3 million Canadian Distance-Learning Development Centre, a consortium of Athabasca University, AT & T Canada, Alberta Government Telephones, ACCESS Alberta (an educational broadcasting agency), and two departments of the government of Alberta. The new corporation is designed to offer what none of the institutions can or chooses to do individually – the design, development and marketing of new responses to the problems of distance delivery using the newest educational technologies. Each partner brings a specific expertise to the table, the notion being that the consequent synthesis will be the genesis of new and commercially viable products and services. This sort of organization makes whole new demands on its management, as is discussed below.

One of the classic reasons for collaboration is to widen the base of political support for an idea or service, and it is the *raison d'être* for political parties, trade unions, lobby groups and all sorts of consortia and associations, such as the Western Canadian Consortium of University Distance Educators (WCCUDE), Ontario's Contact North, and the Canadian Association for Distance Education (CADE), all in Canada; the Australian and South Pacific External Studies Association (ASPESA); the EADTU (European Association of Distance Teaching Universities); the International Council for Distance Education (ICDE), and the Commonwealth of Learning.

Promotion and marketing also creates internal pressures for collaboration – this follows directly from above. The Alberta government established five educational consortia in five relatively isolated regions of the province too sparsely populated to justify the creation of a college. These serve as pressure groups on the universities and colleges to respond to local needs and also as promotional vehicles for courses and services offered. They do not hire faculty themselves, but instead serve as clearing houses to promote and integrate programme offerings from their member institutions. On a somewhat grander scale, the newly created Commonwealth of Learning, centred in Vancouver, British Columbia, is dedicated to similar goals in the promotion of distance education throughout the Commonwealth of Nations.

Status is sometimes attached to a collaborative venture, especially for an institution which is seen to be collaborating with a better-known or more established institution or in an international project.

The quality of one's own programmes can be challenged (and, one hopes, verified) by exposing them to scrutiny by those in another institution through a collaborative venture. This requires unusual degrees of self-confidence and openness, but the rewards can be considerable if the 'fit' between the two institutions is a good one.

Sometimes the motive for joining with another institution is to reduce the competitive risk. In the previously mentioned CDLDC venture, there is at least some suspicion that one of the partners joined primarily to keep an eye on another's activities in Alberta.

More cynically, institutions have been known to join ventures to ensure that they are not too successful. I will refrain from giving examples here, but we all have our suspicions.

Finally, and I hope it is not the least important reason, collaborative ventures can offer new opportunities to students which would not otherwise exist. Credit-transfer arrangements, college capstone programmes, common admissions banks, and opportunities to study and live in different cultures are several examples in this area.

The impact of personal relationship and informal communications should not be minimized. Many a collaborative arrangement has been started between old friends because of a mutual desire to work together or as an international venture which would give both an opportunity for exotic travel. Some very exciting innovations and not a few disasters have been spawned in this way.

The unintended consequences of collaboration

> Things are seldom what they seem;
> Skim milk masquerades as cream;
> Highlows pass as patent leathers;
> Jackdaws strut in peacock's feathers.
> > Very true,
> > So they do.
> (W S Gilbert, *HMS Pinafore*, Act II)

Many collaborative ventures are more fanfare than reality, and those that are implemented do not always turn out as intended. In fact, most collaborations produce something quite different from the originally stated goals, sometimes for the better and often for the worse. I would cite the following examples and illustrations:

- Large consortia, in particular, often get bogged down in their own operations. There is strong competition to be the 'lead' institution, and, in Merton's classic theory of the displacement of goals,[4] a tendency for the means (the organizational structures and processes) to become ends in themselves, usually to the detriment of the original ends.

- Especially if set up quickly in reaction to something, or casually through informal contacts, collaborative schemes may be very fuzzy in their intentions, mean different things to different partners, and never really get off the ground. What Freeman has termed 'ritual declarations of friendship'[5] may mask hidden agendas and concerns, with the result that negotiations go on for years without tangible result.

- Politics can be costly. The previously mentioned entrepreneurial project spearheaded by Athabasca University will cost about $120,000 of federal government money as a demonstration project in cooperative federalism – the same project conducted by the university alone would cost significantly less and be produced more quickly.

- Sometimes, partners try to make more of an arrangement than was originally intended, so that an information-sharing agency like WCCUDE, for example, is seen as a source of power for taking over a share of a market. This will be highly resisted by other partners, however, especially those who may have joined precisely to stop this sort of takeover.

- All the problems of management, notably those in leading course teams, for example, are exacerbated by institutional distance. Paul's First Law of Collaboration, derived from some of my own recent experiences, suggests that the difficulty of managing a consortium increases exponentially with every new partner.

- There are significant differences in the cultures of various organizations which render the management of collaborative ventures extremely difficult (although admittedly fascinating at the same time). Again, CDLDC's marriage of government, industry and universities is supposed to produce the best of each – public responsibility and funds (government), entrepreneurship (industry), and creativity and innovation (university). The danger is that it will produce instead, the speed of government, the public responsibility of industry, and the decision-making models of universities.

- Collaboration sometimes becomes more difficult as it becomes more specific. It is usually easier to agree about general principles and grand schemes than it is to work out the details of who has what authority and who does all the work. Paul's Second Law of Collaboration is that interinstitutional agreement is more likely the higher one goes in the organization. Hence, presidents will agree to almost anything with each other, vice-presidents will usually find a way through, while deans are much more sceptical. Faculty are strongly resistant, and academic secretaries don't want to know!

- Freeman[6] has noted the problems of collaboration if the stages of development of two or more institutions are very different. This is particularly a problem with international ventures, although it may be a problem of perception more than reality, when the institution from a developed country completely underestimates the stage of development of a newly created, Third-World institution.

- Again following Freeman,[7] the intensity of collaboration is an important variable. Presumably, the less the intensity, the more likely the collaborative effort is to become diffuse and to fail. While it may yet come about, some of the original impetus for an official relationship between the major distance-education units of the Republic of Ireland and Northern Ireland has been lost, at least in part because there has been more goodwill than urgency in the discussions which have spanned almost a decade.

The early history of the previously mentioned Canadian Distance-Learning Development Centre in Alberta makes an excellent case study to illustrate some of the above concerns. Launched with much enthusiasm and fanfare in 1987, with the multimillion dollar support of the government of Alberta, CDLDC's early euphoria for an exciting, future-orientated technological concept of education apparently masked strong disagreements about the purpose, mandate and governance of the institution.

Even two years after its establishment, there was no clear consensus as to whether its central mission was research or product development and marketing; debates over this originated in the politics of which organizations were in control and the personalities of key players. A major difficulty, not atypical of entrepreneurial ventures, was the high turnover in key personnel, which restricted the development of an organizational culture and of a top team committed to a common view of the agency and its mission. As a result, issues were frequently redebated, sometimes with different outcomes as new players contradicted the viewpoints of their predecessors. Commitment to the consortium was not very high in any of the organizations, except among the few key executives who had spawned CDLDC in the first place, some of whom were no longer involved because of new responsibilities within or outside their original affiliations.

The membership of CDLDC was determined before it was absolutely clear what contribution each partner would make to the overall concept. It is easy to criticize this in hindsight, but, of course, a major factor in the original conception was political clout to raise the requisite resources and corporate profile.

The different cultures of a private corporation, two government agencies and a university also made it difficult to forge a common identity and style of operation within the new entity. While, generally speaking, the private-sector participants wanted to move the most quickly, and the government representatives the most carefully, there were occasional role reversals, and everyone blamed everyone else for the inaction, the lack of clear strategic and business planning, and the confusion over how the CDLDC should operate.

Moreover, CDLDC initially tried to achieve too much through its board and committees, which were made up of senior managers from the consortium members. While most had high enthusiasm for the concept, they all had higher priorities and responsibilities within their own organizations, necessitating the engagement of a full-time president. This was achieved about one year after the organization was established, but the incumbent soon found that there remained considerable confusion and disagreement about priorities and objectives. This manifested itself in a number of unfortunate ways, notably in contradictory messages from the board and management committees, who expected the president to provide strong leadership but did not always agree in which direction.

This illustration is not atypical of this sort of venture. More than two years after its foundation, there are signs that CDLDC is beginning to live up to the promise it has always held. After several policy reversals, research has been clearly established as its primary function, and the separation of policy-making and executive functions is much clearer. No one dares claim that any of this has been achieved easily.

It is easy to suggest ways in which CDLDC could have been more effectively established. What is much more important is to recognize that good new ideas are not always simple to implement, that the process of coping with the growing pains is often a very productive one and that managers from all sectors need to learn how to function in project-based organizations. Patience, flexibility, persistence, and retaining an overall vision while making the inevitable adjustments to the original concepts are attributes essential to the success of such an initiative.

Cultural differences also pose particular challenges for the management of international ventures. Athabasca University has been involved in a fascinating development project in northeast Thailand for the past five years in collaboration with the huge Rhamkhamhaeng University. Through the hard work of dedicated staff in both institutions, the project seems to be a very successful one, but it is by no means the same project that the Canadian participants had in mind when they first visited Thailand in 1985. Earlier simplistic notions of the Canadian institution lending its expertise to the less developed Thai institution have been replaced by growing recognition that, if anything, it is the Canadians who have learned from the Thais.

This lesson reinforces the value of international collaboration, which can be quite beneficial to both parties. The unique Rhamkhamhaeng system of electing senior administrators every two years has rendered it difficult to establish the sorts of personal relationships which are crucial to the success of such ventures. Despite three completely different administrations at the Thai university in five years, relationships between Rhamkhamhaeng and Athabasca are extremely good, but, again, it has required unusual fortitude, persistence and belief in the project from key people on both sides of the Pacific for this to occur.

Lessons for collaboration

It follows from the above that a collaborative venture has a greater likelihood of success if:

- A clear benefit is established for and understood by each member party.
- The objectives of the collaborative venture are clearly spelled out, and specific schedules and measures of achievement are set out and agreed to by all partners.
- Clear objectives and schedules notwithstanding, both (all) parties recognize that these may have to be reconsidered and renegotiated on a number of occasions as they understand each other's cultures and objectives better, and as the environment changes. Flexibility is essential, but it must be within the context of the original, overall goals of the venture.
- The consortium involves the fewest members required to achieve its objectives. Ideally, the arrangement is bilateral rather than multilateral (see Paul's First Law above).
- Clear authority and responsibility are delegated to specific individuals, using such mechanisms as interinstitutional steering committees only for broad questions of policy and direction. If the collaborative agency is large enough, those responsible for implementation should be different from those responsible for overall policy and direction.
- Understanding and taking into account the respective corporate cultures is seen as an important and valuable activity and one which may lead to very real and positive change in one or other of the partner institutions.
- The venture is scrutinized on a regular basis and disbanded if its original goals are achieved or if significant goal displacement has taken place. Too often, such agreements are perpetuated far beyond their original usefulness.
- The agreements have the full support of the chief executive officer of

each partner, as demonstrated by clear and firm commitments of human and other resources from the outset.

All the above notwithstanding, cooperative ventures are essential to the long-term success of open universities and lie at the heart of their commitment to adult education and lifelong learning. It just that they need to demonstrate that commitment to open learning, not only in the objectives of collaborative ventures, but in the way that they run them as well.

Notes

1. Paul, R H (1989), 'Lessons from Collaboration in Distance Education in Western Canada', paper presented at 'Recent Trends in Adult Education', Centre for Canadian Studies, Queen's University, Belfast, May (to be published in conference proceedings).
2. See, for example, Callahan, J (1986), 'Chemistry: How Mismatched Managements Can Kill a Deal', *Mergers and Acquisitions,* March–April, pp 47–53; Kitching, J (1967), 'Why Do Mergers Miscarry?', *Harvard Business Review,* Nov–Dec, pp 84–101; and Levinson, H (1970), 'A Psychologist Diagnoses Merger Failures', *Harvard Business Review,* March–April, pp 20–8 (from an unpublished annotated bibliography by Carol Beatty, Queen's University).
4. Merton, R K (1952), 'Bureaucratic Structure and Personality' in Merton, R K et al (ed), *Reader in Bureaucracy,* Glencoe, Illinois: Free Press, p 365.
5. Freeman, R (1981), 'Collaboration in Distance Learning' in Neil, M W (ed), *Education of Adults at a Distance,* London: Kogan Page, p 146.
6. Ibid, p 173.
7. Ibid, p 148.

CHAPTER 10

The Day-to-Day Challenges of Management
– When Context Gets in the Way

Chapter synopsis

As with everything else, we judge our leaders by what they do on a day-to-day basis, not what they say. In this chapter, the pious pronouncements on value-driven leadership are challenged by some of the most difficult and frequent occurrences that face every manager, those moments when scarce resources and individual human concerns upset the best-laid plans.

The real test of value-driven leadership comes not in periods of expansion when resources are plentiful and everyone's needs can be addressed, but in fiscally tighter times when resources are scarce, and tough choices have to be made among competing priorities. Ironically though, some of the worst management decisions, the ones which have the greatest long-term impact on the organization, are made in prosperity when managers are more apt to be careless and sloppy; going through tougher times can greatly improve the quality of management in an institution. These issues are explored in terms of annual budget decisions and their implications for staff relations. The latter concern is pursued further by looking at a number of interpersonal matters too seldom addressed in books about management and administration.

Whenever someone conducts a survey of administrators to compare what they say they do to how they actually spend their time, the differences are startling.[1] People tend to overestimate the time they spend on conceptualization, team-building, external liaison and planning, and to underestimate the hours spent on administrivia, procrastination, getting organized and talking informally to colleagues.

No matter how well organized and prepared the individual, much management time is spent reacting to sudden problems, trying to understand hidden agendas and otherwise attending to problems and activities not originally on the day's or week's schedule. While managers themselves can do much to avoid this tendency to 'firefight' or 'manage by crisis', not even the best can anticipate everything; besides, a lot of this activity is important to effective leadership.

In this section, some of the most frequent and important such influences are explored as 'context' that keeps 'getting in the way' of the best-laid plans. In short, it deals with what happens when daily life gets in the way of management. The point is that the needs, aspirations and concerns of individuals are not neatly assembled in manageable packages, but influence perceptions, reactions and decisions in many different ways and often at inopportune times.

This has been recognized by many organizational theorists for some time, especially in reacting to the structural–functional school which has long dominated the field. The Ethnomethodological and phenomeno-logical approaches which developed in the late 1960s and early 1970s were particularly useful in exposing the limitations of the grand theories of organization and management which had been dominant until then.[2] The care and concern such theorists take to understand the motivations and perceptions of individuals in micro-situations is particularly attractive to the practising administrator and has led to a more self-critical approach to organizational management.

In recognizing the validity of this approach, this chapter deals with a number of issues which may seem rather loosely assembled and not necessarily directly related. Nevertheless, the way an institutional manager handles these sorts of concerns will probably have more to do with his or her success on the job than the sum total of management theory, and, in this sense at least, all of the following issues are directly related.

Fiscal management in 'good' and 'bad' times

Whatever institutional leaders say they stand for and whatever their public mission statements and proclamations of goals and objectives for their institutions, the true test of their values and priorities is how resources are allocated in their institution – whose staffing requests are filled, who gets the new capital equipment and space, and which units seem always to have extra flexibility in responding to new needs.

In the ideal institution, as discussed in more detail in Chapter 11, there are no contradictions among an institution's mission statement, its long-range plan, its strategic plan and the decisions of its budget com-mittee. In reality, personalities, power struggles, pressure groups, time constraints, insufficient or inaccurate information and outright incom-petence all conspire against the ideal.

DEFINING 'GOOD' AND 'BAD' TIMES

On the face of it, distinguishing between 'good' and 'bad' fiscal times should not be difficult. 'Good' times can be defined as those when there are sufficient additional resources to permit the institution to embark on new ventures and/or expand existing ones without sacrificing any commitments to existing initiatives, programmes and services. 'Bad' times are defined as those when the resources available are significantly less than the minima required to achieve one's current objectives, let alone cope with expansion or support new initiatives.

In practice, the difference between 'good' and 'bad' in this context is not nearly as clear cut, but is, in fact, both relative and subjective, the situation being very much in the eye of the beholder. Obviously, context is important here. It is patronizing to discuss relativity for an institution in a Third-World country which lacks resources absolutely basic to its central tasks. It is also easier to accept that tough times are relative rather than absolute when the duration of a period of recession is relatively short (one or two years) rather than extended. However, while some of what follows may be less appropriate to institutions in a poorer country, the fact that Third-World institutions do so much with so little, actually reinforces the assertion that differences between good and bad in this context are relative and subjective. (I first really appreciated this when I visited Ramkhamhaeng University in Thailand in 1986 and discovered that its registrar's office was one-fifth the size of Athabasca's even though serving 700 times as many students!)

My own move from Quebec to Alberta underlines this point. My tenure as academic dean at Dawson College coincided with some difficult years in terms of fiscal support and labour relations as the institution faced enrolment declines and a totally enrolment-driven budget which forced consideration of staff lay-offs. The impact of this on decision-making has already been described (see pp 33–4 above).

I came from this relatively difficult period to a province still benefiting from the high prosperity of a boom in oil prices. My last budget in Quebec had involved a significant cut in the institution's operating budget, while my first few years in Alberta were rewarded with budget increases of 10 per cent and more, the most extreme case being a 49 per cent budget increase for Athabasca University in a year when we didn't even request that much. (It should be noted that this had much to do with the forced relocation of the university from Edmonton to the tiny town of Athabasca, 100 miles north, so that it was seen as not only 'gilt' money but also 'guilt' money.) Nevertheless, my first Athabasca University budget in Alberta, with major increases in grants, was no less onerous than my last in Quebec, with significant cuts, because the booming Alberta economy raised local aspirations for resources to levels which no budget could satisfy.

However, having made the point about the relativity of budget cuts,

I will now compare management under two separate scenarios in Alberta and how decision-making related to the value-driven leadership advocated throughout this book.

MANAGING IN 'GOOD' TIMES

To keep things in perspective, there should be no doubt that most managers prefer good times to bad ones. (There are always a few who seem genuinely to enjoy gloominess, although one suspects it has more to do with their own power needs than any genuine masochism.) While one can take great pride in the way that an institution copes with severe cutbacks without apparent loss of service or initiative, for most people, it is even more rewarding successfully to implement a new programme, provide better service to clients or expand an already successful operation to new client groups. It is the difference between doing well a job that *has* to be done and one that one *wants* to do.

Management is fun in good times. The manager's powers are enhanced by his or her ability to dole out financial and other resources in support of good ideas, and there is greater scope for directly rewarding those who have produced through salary increments and bonuses. Money spent on staff development and team building can improve morale and give everyone a lot of confidence in the effectiveness and productivity of the organization.

The problem is, and it seems to happen almost inevitably with time, the extra resources available in periods of prosperity can be used to avoid the sorts of choices and decisions that managers are forced to make in less affluent times – instead of choosing between competing priorities, one can support them both.

An analogy with canoe tripping comes to mind. It is easy to be a 'good' canoe tripper when the weather is sunny. One can go to bed on a messy campsite with wood strewn all over the place, tents badly put up or poorly located and food unprotected, and still wake up the next morning with impunity. If there is rain, however, wood that is not stored away will get wet and be difficult to light in the morning, and a tent may blow down or be soaked if trenches aren't dug; or the food may be raided by animals. As for canoe trippers, good management practised in good times will serve the university well during the bad ones.

While it is based only on casual observation rather than documented research, it seems to me that planning documents emerging from institutions during good times are less rigorous than those associated with bad times in that they are far less apt to establish clear priorities among competing demands. Instead, they incorporate everyone's 'wish list' and leave it to some other undetermined body or official to set priorities. Typical of this was Athabasca University's Long-Range Plan, developed during the more affluent early 1980s, an interesting and ambitious document which was almost completely inoperable because it stipulated no priorities and made no provision for new resources in support of the proposed initiatives. The university's Strategic Academic Plan, emerging from a much tougher budget, established absolute priorities, implementation deadlines, and evaluation benchmarks, and addressed the issues of resource allocation and fund-raising in support of these priorities.

The government of Alberta, during one particularly prosperous period, approved hundreds of proposals for new university and college programmes to clear a backlog of requests. This was done by ministerial pronouncement, with very little of the usual scrutiny of new programmes to ensure that they were well designed, complemented others in the system and could be funded permanently. While the results were very positive for many new initiatives, some very bad decisions resulted as well – programmes for which there was almost no student demand, programmes which were far more expensive than had been anticipated, and programmes for which there was no labour supply. Departmental officials still regret many of those decisions, especially as they have had to turn down much better proposals more recently because of shortages of resources.

MANAGING IN 'BAD' TIMES

While managing in 'bad' times may not be as much 'fun', it can be very rewarding and also lead to structures and processes which serve the institution better when the fiscal situation improves. An institutional leader has some advantages in tougher fiscal climates. It is usually easier to convince others that the situation is serious, and there is more institutional tolerance of strict measures which would be vigorously opposed in more prosperous settings.

A major variable is how the leader presents the situation. Open communications, good documentation and a frank presentation of what the institution is facing will usually pay dividends as others learn to accept the fiscal difficulties and take them as a challenge to overcome. This will be completely undermined, however, if the leader is seen as manufacturing or overstating the 'crisis' for his or her own ends. There will not be much tolerance for a leader who asks staff to make deep cuts when there is obviously a lot of money elsewhere for more frivolous things, or for one who has been guilty of 'crying wolf' in the past.

One strategy, popular in many universities in earlier times, is deliberately to adopt a deficit in anticipation of better times ahead. This is a first-class recipe for disaster and one to be avoided at almost all costs. There still are examples of governments bailing out institutions with large deficits, but as a deliberate strategy, it is irresponsible and unnecessary. No matter how expansionary and innovative the vision, a leader must under no circumstances deliberately allow a base deficit. More frequently, institutions fall into deficit financing unwittingly, often because of poor decision-making in better times. It is astounding how many senior managers of universities, and, one assumes, other organizations, ignore the differences between 'soft' and 'hard' money in decision-making. For example, many universities make 'permanent' commitments to staff, underlined by clauses in their collective agreements, which are funded by external grants or other sources of revenue that are not part of the institution's base budget. When the external programme suddenly folds, the institution is left with an expensive problem.

Another source of difficulty, which usually arises in good times but doesn't become obvious until the bad times, is the assumption that the way things have always been done is the way they must continue to be done. This can lead very dangerously to a fatalistic acceptance of major fiscal problems as if they are out of everyone's control. I encountered much of this kind of thinking at Britain's Open University when people shrugged off financial problems as ones caused by more students taking up their places than in previous years (as if the institution had no control over how many students enrolled). In my experience, problems attributed entirely to the external environment or other factors outside staff control are never properly addressed and the essential first step for their resolution is to take full responsibility for them.

It is easy to make these points on paper and much harder to live by them on the job. One important strategy is to have a more open budget process, one which delegates far more responsibility to line managers for their own budgeting and expenditure. As long as fiscal control is seen as 'their' (meaning the vice-chancellor and chief financial officer) rather than 'our' problem, the institution will almost certainly encounter serious financial difficulties.

It is not difficult to make it abundantly clear that each manager has full responsibility for staying within the budget, no matter what the circumstances. It helps to offer incentives on the positive side, such as a small percentage carry-over to the next fiscal year for managers who have managed to achieve their objectives without deploying all their resources as long as there is some equity in the original resource distribution.

It should not be concluded from this analysis that the answer lies completely in delegation down the ranks, for those at the most senior level have the 'biggest picture' and sometimes the only way out of a tough fiscal position is strong, centralized decision-making. For example, a staff 'freeze' (a moratorium on hiring for vacant positions) is a useful short-term device to deliver a strong message to an institution and to give the president some room for manoeuvre in facing financial difficulties, but it is not the sort of measure which will normally emerge by consensus of those whom it affects directly. Strong and even precipitous action is sometimes essential, but it will always be more effective if those subjected to it at least understand both the general institutional context and its specific rationale at the time it is taken.

CONCLUSION: MANAGING IN ALL SEASON

There really should not be a major difference between how we manage in 'good' or 'bad' times. The main recommendation here is to be more optimistic in tougher times and more pessimistic in easier times.

There are many different budget processes which will achieve the sorts of objectives advocated above. The most important criterion is openness, not in the sense that everyone participates in every decision, but that the process is well known and that decision-making authority is absolutely clear. Hallmarks of a good budget process, then, are:

- It is closely attached to strategic planning (see Chapter 11, pp 178–82).
- Subject to such formal authorities as boards of governors or government regulation, the chief executive officer, not the senior financial officer, assumes full and final responsibility for all fiscal decisions.
- There is a clear and thorough process of consultation, emanating from long-range and strategic planning.
- Those responsible for the administration of budgets have ample opportunity to defend their submissions and to ensure that decision-makers are clear about the implications of various cuts or additions.
- Once established, a budget is adhered to for the balance of the fiscal period (reallocations for unanticipated needs should be from funds set aside for that purpose, or by decision of the appropriate manager within already allocated funds).
- Future staff commitments should be fully costed in the year of award so that there are no 'surprises' in the next budget year. This is fiscal conservatism, but the 'soft' funds generated in the present year can be used to provide some flexibility within the formal budget.
- No permanent commitments should be made on 'soft' funds – this is probably the biggest source of difficulty in the future. If permitted, there is a blackmail strategy that can be quite effective here – use 'soft' money to start a service or function which then becomes so integral a part of operations that a future budget committee *has* to fund it.

Labour relations in 'good' and 'bad' times

The fiscal position of an institution is a major variable in labour relations. Senior managers tend to ignore professional associations and
trade unions in good times and then suddenly have to deal with them in
tougher fiscal periods when budget cuts and staff lay-offs and redundan-
cies come under consideration. Good times bring decentralization and
delegation, while bad times invite more centralization and autocracy. In
good times, managers reward people with all sorts of perquisites and in
tough times, they seem to forget reward systems.

However, just as poor fiscal management in good times can yield
major problems in tough times, it is important to pay as much attention
to labour relations in good times as in bad. Regular and open consultation with trade-union and association leaders can build up a climate of
trust and cooperation that will serve the institution well when a crisis
arises. However, university officials should have no illusions about this.
The job of a trade union or association is to represent its members, and
too many administrators have felt badly let down by union leaders
whom they perceive as unappreciative of past favours when tougher
decisions have to be made. This can lead to an overreaction and fast
deterioration in what were apparently good relationships. This is best
countered by maturity on both sides, a recognition that collective bargaining is an excellent decision-making tool.

Queen's University labour-relations specialist Jeffrey Gandz has
developed a useful model for good collective bargaining based on his
experience as a professional mediator.[3] He classifies all items of dispute
between two sides as emanating from one of three sources:

- conflict of interest – where there will be winners and losers;
- common problems – where both sides can win (as in helping an
  employee who is an alcoholic);
- Misunderstandings – pseudoconflict situations.

The first task is to identify items under dispute and to allocate them
among the three categories. There will be some for which this is much
more difficult, as when one side sees as a conflict of interest something
which the other would depict as a misunderstanding. The process of
categorizing is in itself useful in resolving disputes, nevertheless.

The strategy is then quite straightforward – to deal first with common
problems so that genuine progress is made, then to clarify misunderstandings, and finally – and only then – to deal with the genuine
conflicts of interest. If the first two stages are conducted effectively, a
more open and trusting relationship will have developed which may

then encourage the two sides to make trade-offs on the major items of dispute.

Much more difficult to handle are disputes over staff productivity and performance. The issue is usually personalized, and there is a higher likelihood of fundamentally differing viewpoints between labour and management as to the source of the problem (or, indeed, whether there is even a problem at all). Nevertheless, the same patient, open and fair approach that is the hallmark of effective negotiations applies with equal importance here, for an administration must always consider the long-term effect on staff performance and staff relations in each particular case.

Ensuring good labour relations can be a very time-consuming process, but it is worth every minute. While the primary emphasis should be on good communications and positive staff relations which minimize the amount of time spent on disputes, there will inevitably be specific cases of recalcitrance which must be confronted if standards are to be established and maintained. In such cases, the typically endless hours spent in committee, in negotiation and in seeking and considering legal advice, are well justified in terms of longer-term staff performance (and morale, for a tough, fair and even approach to staff performance will be respected by staff more than will one which is perhaps less rigorous but applied less evenly). Good legal advice and careful attention to process are absolutely essential. (The overwhelming conclusion from my own experience in such matters is that, in the great majority of disputes involving performance or tenure at a university, there is usually a good case for disciplinary action, but that more management charges are dismissed for reasons of process than of substance.

A very typical case in a university illustrates the point about the good times setting the tone for the bad. Far too often, in earlier and more affluent times, universities paid very little attention to faculty accountability, performance review and criteria for tenure and promotion. In tighter fiscal climates, however, where there are few vacancies and greater expectations for workload and performance, administrations are much more active in confronting poor performance and incompetence. The problem is that, if a staff member has received satisfactory (or even exemplary) performance ratings during a long period of low productivity, it is extremely difficult suddenly to build a case for dismissal given the fundamental principle that an employee deserves fair indication of concern about performance and a reasonable time to adjust to the expectations of the employer.

However great the claim on a manager's time, an effective process of consultation and decision-making will yield dividends in the future, and, conversely, a poorly handled case will lead to a far greater (and less productive) consumption of time in the future.

Another important variable in labour relations is the management of change. It is much easier to cope with change when one is the initiator, and much more difficult when one is the object of the change. More and more frequently, change is being initiated by management, and hence trade unions are usually in the position of reacting to this.[4]Again, an open environment where surprises are kept to a minimum and union leaders are kept well informed as to plans and their rationales can assist management in implementing change and need not necessarily be at the expense of its power and authority.

Finally, collective bargaining over salaries and benefits should be no less rigorous in good times. Staff members have every right to an appropriate share of additional resources, but this should not be at the expense of the institution's priorities. So-called surpluses should be earmarked for specific priorities (see pp 178–82 on strategic planning in Chapter 11). Administrations which allow additional revenues to be allocated to salaries without concomitant improvements in productivity will have a more difficult time cutting salaries in tougher times, and may quickly find themselves stuck with an organizational model which they cannot afford.

Strong investment in good staff relations, then, will usually yield very positive results in the long term. Inattention to this matter or uneven and ill-considered handling of individual cases can lead to serious-labour-relations issues which make far greater demands on management time than an original investment in the particular case would have required. There can be few better examples of the old adage, 'short-term pain for long-term gain'!

Things they don't write about in management texts

My college Terry Morrison, President of Athabasca University, has often remarked that some of the biggest challenges in management are those not usually dealt with in management texts, and he suggested addressing a few of these in this book. At the risk of demonstrating why others have chosen not to write about such matters. I have selected a few of my personal favourites. Most of the issues involve personal relationships or perceptions of the same. Their common characteristic is that they are usually underlying concerns which have a major, if unstated, impact on employee performance and decision-making in institutions and hence require the attention and skill of any competent manager. The most prevalent include the following:

Home-based problems. Staff members face personal problems and stress which interfere with their work effectiveness – conflict and disruption in their marriage or family, illness or death in the family, trouble with their children, financial pressures, or other changes in their personal circumstances. Everyone experiences these, and an effective manager is one who is not only tolerant and supportive of employees in times of strife but also sensitive to their emotions and concerns at all times. It is equally important for the manager to recognize his or her own symptoms of stress, to become expert at coping with it, but also to acknowledge it openly when stress is interfering with his or her own performance. A small amount of time invested in informal chats with key staff each week can pay rich dividends for a manager in terms of developing a mutually supportive atmosphere in the office or unit.

Requests for special treatment. Whether handicapped, single parents, or having to cope with major family problems, some employees request special dispensations – time off, different hours, or other favours. The challenge for managers is to know how tolerant to be, trying to treat all employees fairly while recognizing that some inevitably take advantage of leniency here. An organization with a clear philosophy and policies on these matters can greatly assist managers and ensure more even treatment across departments, especially where there is a good relationship between the administration and staff unions or associations. Of particular importance are 'arms-length' counselling, alcohol and drug abuse programmes which provide both employee assistance and education for managers and staff alike, while recognizing the individual's right to confidentiality and privacy in the process.

'Trivial' issues that are important. Every organization has policy and staff-relations issues which seem relatively trivial but are nevertheless critical to the establishment of the organizational climate and culture. Among the most frequent are policies on smoking and nonsmoking, access to parking, and the provision of time and facilities for coffee, meals and leisure activities. It would be interesting to log the number of hours executive groups of almost any organization have spent on such issues, as compared to more apparently major items like the institution's strategic plan (a local university has a 25-page booklet of parking regulations!). The irony is that much of the time input is a result of not taking the issue seriously enough at the outset and not recognizing its importance to organizational health and staff morale. The most effective approach is to deal with each issue openly, consulting widely and sharing decision-making responsibility with employee groups, but moving as quickly as possible to clear-cut decisions which can put the issue to rest until there are new problems or changes which have to be addressed.

Personal relationships at work. Office relationships have always posed difficulties, but they are probably even more prevalent and certainly more evident in today's more open society. Athabasca University's unique circumstances, whereby the entire university was moved to a small and relatively isolated town, has exacerbated this problem to the extent that an unusually high proportion of staff are intermarried and spousal employment opportunity has been a major issue in the recruitment of staff from elsewhere. As one who has experienced this one from both sides (as a manager and as someone married to another staff member), I have always found this difficult to deal with. Two observations stand out on the basis of my own experience – no matter how hard couples try to avoid even a hint of conflict of interest in decision-making, others will always assume the worst, and, more fundamentally, it will almost always be the woman's career which suffers the most. The answer is not to legislate against office relationships but to deal with perceived problems openly and sympathetically while avoiding direct-reporting relationships or same-department employment as much as possible.

Confidentiality. Perhaps universities, especially small ones, are more prone to abuse of this than some other sorts of organizations, but my experience has been that very little remains confidential in an organization. The supposedly private deliberations of committees involved in hiring decisions, grievances or dismissals are quickly public knowledge, to the point that other staff know not only of behind-the-doors decisions but also who voted which way and why. Strict confidentiality should be the rule here, to protect the integrity of the process and the reputations of individuals. However, where knowledge is the currency of power, gossip will always prevail, and the solution is not to hurl accusations or go on witch-hunts for those who violated confidentiality. The emphasis should be on the positive – it is incumbent upon the institution's leadership to provide models of decorum and integrity, and to insist on confidentiality on appropriate occasions, and both individuals and groups should take pride in their ability to retain confidences.

'Trying' people in the halls. This refers not to difficult people roaming the halls, but to the prevalence of institutional gossip which decides in advance of any fair assessment that someone is incompetent, guilty of a misdemeanour or not worthy of promotion or tenure. Institutions have formal processes to determine whether or not there is just cause for such allegations, and these must be applied thoughtfully and carefully where a case cannot otherwise be resolved. Moral indignation is an easy passion to arouse (I can remember several hundred faculty at Dawson

College signing a petition against something one day and then scrambling to have their names removed the next when they learned new facts about the issue), but it is not well served by an administration which is seen to overreact to the latest crisis, or to be unduly swayed by a particular prevailing opinion.

Duration of tenure in management positions. I firmly believe that leaders outlive their usefulness in given positions and given organizations. Given that every individual has strengths and weaknesses, one can assume that long after the former have contributed to the organization, the latter will remain, and problems will persist. Hence, I favour term-specific appointments to senior administrative posts in a university (deanships, vice-presidencies, presidencies), preferably five-year renewable terms, a second renewal requiring a more open external competition to encourage ten years as the usual maximum, but I would allow for a longer term where the individual continues to be outstanding or where the job or institution have changed dramatically during the incumbent's tenure. There is a lot to be gained from new blood at the top, no matter how effective the old regime has been, for even the shake-up itself can be healthy in forcing the organization to 'unfreeze' somewhat and to redefine its priorities and plans.

New hirings which just do not work out. No matter how experienced and successful a manager is, he or she will make hiring decisions that just don't seem to work out as well as anticipated, even after every effort has been made to assist the new employee or to make appropriate changes in assignments and expectations. Too often, managers are very defensive about this, and sometimes they do not deal in a forthright matter with their 'mistakes'. The effective manager will act on such matters quickly and decisively, given that every reasonable prior effort has been made to resolve problems. Hiring decisions are probably the most important ones taken by managers, and it is important to foster a climate in the organization which provides as much assistance to them as possible, but also one which is nonpunitive and encourages them to learn from past failures in this area.

These are just some of the sorts of problems and issues encountered on a daily basis by institutional managers. It is difficult to be prescriptive, because every issue has its own particular dimensions and personal ingredients. The major points to be made here are the following:

- Such issues are not secondary to institutional success. How managers deal with them will define the culture and climate of the organization.

- My own approach is to be quite liberal in designing flexible work patterns and policies which take into account the personal circumstances, work habits and skills of individuals. This approach notwithstanding, the job must ultimately come first, and the flexibility must be balanced by clear and firm standards about what is expected of employees.
- Very often, work problems, frequent illness or attitude problems are symptoms of deeper difficulties. A manager who is a good and sympathetic listener will perceive these symptoms quickly and hence be able to help an employee to deal with them, or refer him or her to appropriate treatment and support.

How a manager deals with the sorts of issues discussed above will reveal more than anything else his or her true value system. The process of open management advocated in this book will render the leader more exposed and vulnerable on occasion than do more directive or political styles, but, it is argued, a value-driven approach which is open and consistent over a period of time will ultimately contribute to an organizational climate which is more productive and conducive to coping with unpredictable change.

Notes

1. See, for example, Noon, J (1985), *'A' Time: The Busy Manager's Action Plan for Effective Self-Management*, Wokingham, Berkshire: Van Nostrand Reinhold (UK) Ltd, p 17.
2. A useful example is Silverman, D (1970), *The Theory of Organisations: A Sociological Framework*, London: Heinemann.
3. From notes presented at The Executive Programme, Queen's University, Kingston, Ontario, 30 June, 1989.
4. Kochen, T A and Cappelli, P (1983), 'The Transformation of the Industrial Relations and Personnel Function' in Osterman, P (ed), *Employment Policies of Large Firms*, New York: MIT Press, p 1.

Part 4: Looking to the Future: The Search for Leadership

This concluding section looks at the future: its key issues and challenges and the kinds of leader and leadership skills which will be required.

CHAPTER 11

Leadership, Integrity and the Future

Chapter synopsis

In coping with both continuous and discontinuous change, organizations require strong leadership and cultures which make them 'learning' organizations. This chapter offers some personal viewpoints on many facets of institutional leadership in today's society and on some of the mechanisms and techniques which can assist leaders of open-learning institutions, notably strategic planning, institutional marketing and staff development. The last section offers some lessons from the management of open learning for the future – lessons of organizations, of education, and of management and leadership.

Within the context of open learning, this book has focused on the theory and practice of management and institutional leadership in an increasingly complex world. After an analysis of the sorts of leadership which will be required, this chapter examines several of the key tools available to today's leaders, how they can be applied effectively in the management of open learning, and some general lessons that can be learned from the foregoing.

The search for leadership

WELCOMING CHANGE: THE 'LEARNING' ORGANIZATION

In the face of rapid and unpredictable change, society has a greater need for leadership than ever before. This constant change, both continuous and discontinuous, coupled with a more open society than in previous eras, makes leadership more difficult and leaders more vulnerable. It is no surprise that there is widespread cynicism in our society about our leaders, whether they be in politics, business or higher education.

For organizational leaders, it is increasingly difficult but no less critical to maintain a sense of purpose and direction in the face of such change. Tom Peters has stated this quite emphatically:

> To meet the demands of the fast-changing competitive scene, we must
> simply learn to love change as much as we have hated it in the past.[1]

The answer is not in any one technique or process but in an overt and
fundamental commitment to coping with, and even thriving on, change
throughout the organization. The challenge is to develop an atmosphere
that is always ready for change, an institution that is alert and responsive, but one where it is also recognized that coping with change requires
self-confidence and security and a strong belief in what the organization
is doing. As Morrison has stated it, we must think of our institutions as
'learning organizations':

> If learning is the *raison d'être* of open-learning systems, then organiza-
> tions involved in that process should be learning organizations.[2]

Responsibility for this must start at the top with the chief executive
officer. He or she will have to develop a clear and bold institutional
direction and communicate it throughout the organization and beyond.
No less critically, the successful leader will ensure the quality of management necessary to realize it within the contextual limitations and
resource constraints that all institutions face.

An appropriate marriage of value-driven leadership and good
political sense is essential to success (as discussed in Chapter 7). While
there are some basic and fundamental values at the heart of any successful organization, no institution can afford the luxury of redebating them
on a regular basis, both because any discussion of basic values can be
divisive and also because it deflects energy away from action. Some
critical decisions must be made at the outset, and they will not be easily
or painlessly made, but once the directions are defined, the effective
leader will channel energies towards their implementation and only
tolerate debate at the most fundamental value level when it is essential
to the well-being of the organization.

CHALLENGES FOR TOMORROW: WHAT KINDS OF LEADERS WILL BE
NEEDED?

It is in the face of conflict and the 'organized anarchy' of a complex
institution like a university where the real effectiveness of a leader is
tested. A strong sense of purpose and direction are critical, but they
must be assisted by sensitivity to those affected by decisions, good
political judgement (notably in being able to identify the major issues
where intervention is essential and the less important ones which can be

left to internal processes) and, perhaps above all else, a good sense of humour, the sort that comes with strong self-esteem and confidence.

Universities, no less than any other organization, are in search of superheroes to lead them. Most universities looking for presidents these days want someone with at least the following:

- a PhD in a major discipline;
- a strong record of research and publication in that discipline;
- skill in consultative and collegial forms of governance;
- strong leadership skills;
- excellent communications and public-speaking skills;
- experience outside the university sector (private enterprise and/or government);
- proven ability to raise funds;
- excellent managerial abilities – to delegate, and build a strong management team;
- 'staying power' – a 'workaholic' with a 'thick skin';
- family stability – good marriage, the 'right' sort of kids (they don't dare say 'a wife who knows how to entertain', but that's often what they want; they wouldn't dare make the same demands on the husband of a female president).

Occasionally, they actually find such people, but, more often than not, incumbents don't quite live up to expectations. In such cases, they are weighed against bright new applicants, usually from several thousand miles away, and are sometimes found wanting – at least, that is, until the replacement proves even less capable, by which time it is too late to recall the original incumbent.

CHARACTERISTICS OF EFFECTIVE LEADERS

Whatever the specifics of the above requirements, my own experience has suggested that the following characteristics are essential to strong positive leadership. No individual will have them all, but effective leaders have most of the following:

- a clear vision for the organization and the ability to articulate it and inspire commitment to it;
- a passionate belief in the organization and the directions it is pursuing;
- a positive view of people, one holding that people can achieve if they are given the opportunity and support;
- dedication to excellence and the unrelenting pursuit of the organization's goals;

- high self-esteem, and self-knowledge about both strengths and weaknesses, so as to capitalize fully on the former and to compensate for the latter by finding people who are excellent in these areas;
- a sense of humour, integrity and perspective that temper the strong leadership drive with sensitivity to colleagues, and the ability to lead a happy life, both on and off the job;
- a commitment to learning and change, first of all for his or her own lifelong development, and, secondly, for the organization.

While it is not usually associated with leadership, I believe that there is no more important characteristic than the ability to laugh at oneself, to put current problems into perspective and to ensure that whatever is achieved is achieved openly and fairly, with respect always given to (and therefore probably emanating from) those whose views did not prevail on the given issue.

A sense of humour has many manifestations, not all of them always conducive to institutional leadership. Whether it is right or not, our society still wants to put its leaders on pedestals, and much of the ritual surrounding government, for example, tends to be intolerant of those who take things less seriously. Following Max Weber's classic analysis of it,[3] charisma and familiarity do not go well together, as humour is so often a vehicle for breaking down rather than building up pomp and circumstance. Indeed, most dictators appear to follow Weber's prescription for combating the instability of charisma by routinizing it through the establishment of social distance and ritual. It is not easy, for example, to retain charisma within one's own family unless relationships are very formal, which brings to mind an oft-quoted remark attributed to Maryon Pearson, the wife of the former Canadian Prime Minister, to the effect that 'behind every famous man stands a surprised woman!'

The role of humour in management is partly a cultural phenomenon, with more traditional, patriarchal societies exhibiting a more serious and formal approach to position and rank. Even in North America, where informality is perhaps most prevalent, leaders are taken (and usually take themselves) quite seriously.

I would like to think that this is changing, that there is not necessarily a contradiction between serious commitment to a mission and the ability to laugh at oneself in the process. It follows from this that we should guard against tendencies towards self-importance and pomposity in management. There is nothing wrong with institutional leaders with big egos; for assuming positions of responsibility and accountability requires strong measures of self-confidence and the ability to withstand a great deal of opposition and stress. It is when such individuals start believing in their self-importance, take privileges way beyond those available to others, and stop listening to others that things begin to go wrong.

CHARACTERISTICS WHICH UNDERMINE LEADERSHIP

Everyone will have his or her own list of characteristics of leaders who are ineffective. On the basis of my own experience and observations of others in leadership roles, I would offer the following behaviours or characteristics as ones which undermine the effectiveness of otherwise competent individuals:

- Uncertainty or confusion about goals and directions – you can't lead if you don't know where you are going.
- An undue sense of self-importance, whereby the so-called leader treats colleagues as subordinates, doesn't know the names of secretaries and clerks, and usually lacks the listening skills requisite to sensitive and effective organizational leadership.
- A leader without a sense of humour – the ability to laugh at one's own foibles and to keep things in perspective. I have worked closely with several individuals who had all the attributes for management except this one, and, in all cases, it thoroughly undermined their effectiveness. On the other hand, I have worked with less talented people whose sense of humour was a redeeming characteristic which made them more effective than their humourless colleagues.
- All talk, no action – while people can be quite inspirational in the short run, we ultimately judge each other by our actions, not our words. Nothing can undermine a leader's effectiveness so quickly as procrastination or decisions which regularly contradict what he or she purports to stand for.
- Insincerity – trust is fundamental to the success of a leader, and it can quickly be undermined by any of the following – giving different messages to different groups, participating in catty gossip (there is a legitimate role for gossip in an institution but it can be a very negative force), or being openly manipulative in almost all dealings with people. A good rule of thumb for combating one's own tendency to gossip is to assume that whatever one says will eventually get back to those who will be less receptive to the message. This keeps one honest and curbs tendencies towards cattiness.
- Insecurity – it is almost impossible to convey a sense of direction and confidence if one is at the same time displaying personal insecurities. Concerns about status, power and how one is being perceived can be very transparent. If the leader demonstrates uncertainty and doubts, how can the followers be expected to have confidence in him or her?

- Playing favourites – the notion of 'loneliness at the top' is not an idle one, for an effective leader must retain some objectivity and 'distance' from the rest of the organization to be effective when crucial decisions must be made. It is thus important that he or she stay in touch with a broad cross-section of the institution and avoid cultivating an 'in' group who wield all the power and receive all the perquisites. This is not to deny the value of cultivating the best people in the institution, but promotions and favours should be, and should be seen to be, dispensed on the basis of demonstrated competence rather than personal relationships or support for the boss's viewpoint. It should also be noted that even the fairest leaders will sometimes be perceived as being unfair, and that, while being sensitive to the perception, the latter should not be unduly concerned about it as long as they believe themselves to be objective and fair.

NEW LEADERSHIP ROLES: WOMEN IN MANAGEMENT

One of the trappings of traditional modes of management is the 'old boys' club', something that is increasingly being challenged, but which nevertheless prevails in most organization. In their 1982 survey of corporations in nine nations in Western Europe, Adler and Izraeli found that fewer than half of the corporations had ever hired a female manager and that 15 per cent of them would not even contemplate it.[4] This is going to change, for both egalitarian and practical reasons.

Far more women should be promoted to senior positions, not only because they deserve the opportunity, but also because of the impact they will have on styles of leadership and the way decisions are made. While I make no claim to being an expert on gender differences, I am convinced that a more equal gender balance in senior management is ultimately in the best interests of almost any organization. The following observations and hypotheses are based on my own experiences in management over the past 15 years:

- Women, by and large, are better listeners and are thus apt to pick up important insights which men may miss.
- Women, by and large, are more sensitive to the feelings and present circumstances of their colleagues, and are thus better readers of nonverbal cues and hidden agendas.
- Probably because most of them have had less experience of team sports than most men, women tend to be less overtly competitive. Competition among men for status, power and authority all too frequently impedes good decision-making in an organization.
- Men's behaviour changes when there are women in the group. At

least in the long run, they will become better listeners and more thoughtful about the impacts of their decisions.

At the same time, women face some major difficulties as they move up the corporate ladder (again, these are offered as hypotheses):

- The male culture, notably that derived from team sports, still drives most organizations and women are often not as experienced or effective in skills valued in this environment, such as 'rah-rah' leadership, public speaking or assertiveness and confrontation.
- Even where a woman's skills equal or exceed a man's, the way she uses them may not be as well received by men, who have been socialized differently.
- Many women still feel guilt or confusion about assuming traditional male roles, especially if they are in any way at the expense of more traditional female roles such as family nurturer. A very common tendency for women, far more than men, is to try to maintain both family and work roles to the point that often threatens burnout.
- There is still tokenism in the promotion of women, just as there is in the promotion of racial minorities in other contexts, and this can sometimes lead individual women to be quite bitter or disillusioned if they ultimately discover that their appointment was based on gender more than perceptions that they were the best qualified for the position (even if they were). Such a perception can also undermine their status and authority in the eyes of others.
- Because it has not been the norm, there are perceptions that staff do not wish to work or do not work as well for women as they do for men.
- Perhaps the difference is best realized at the lower end of the performance scale. There is little question in my own mind that there is usually far more tolerance for a 'difficult' or incompetent male manager than for a female. Perhaps my experience has been skewed, but I see daily examples of male incompetence apparently being overlooked, whereas this is seldom the case for women. It follows that women have to be better qualified than men both to achieve senior management positions and to be recognized as performing them effectively.

There is tangible support for my perceptions in the work of Davidson and Cooper[5] in a British study of 696 female and 195 male managers (supplemented by in-depth interviews with 60 female managers). They found a large number of statistically significant differences between female and male managers. The former were more apt to have conflicting responsibilities between home and career and to have less emotional and domestic support at home; to lack same-sexual role models; to suffer from sexual stereotypes, prejudice and harassment; to have a less flexible management style; to have higher 'Type A', coronary-prone scores on personality tests; and to have a higher total psychosomatic ill-health score. The male managers, on the other hand, were more apt to lack someone to talk to in coping with problems and stress; to be insensitive, and less sympathetic, cooperative or efficient; to have a higher alcohol consumption; and to be unable to produce a satisfactory quantity of work.

Junior and middle-level female managers demonstrated the highest stress levels of all the sample, while the lowest stress was reported by senior male managers.[6] The high stress factors reported by men perhaps reinforce my perception of the impact of competitiveness on male behaviour – they were most bothered by feelings of underpromotion and not being persuasive enough, while female managers were more apt to be concerned about stress factors beyond their control which limited the effectiveness of women in the organization.[7] Similarly, the finding that the women overwhelmingly named confidence building and assertiveness training as their two primary training needs reinforces my perception that women feel relatively powerless in the male culture which characterizes senior management in most organizations.

The promotion of many more women to leadership positions is more than an egalitarian issue, however, for, as Schwartz suggests, 'The sudden, startling recognition that 80% of new entrants in the [US] work force over the next decade will be women, minorities, and immigrants has stimulated a mushrooming incentive to "value diversity".'[8] In other words, corporations will need to gain access to every available talent pool to maintain their competitive advantage in a fast-changing world.

Schwartz goes on to note, however, that the cost of employing women in management is greater than that of employing men, not because of inescapable gender differences but because of conflicts they experience in male-led corporations which produce much higher turnovers among women managers.

> If we are to overcome the cost differential between male and female employees, we need to address the issues that arise when female socialization meets the male corporate culture and masculine rules of career development – issues of behavior and style, of expectation, of stereotypes and preconceptions, of sexual tension and harassment, of female mentoring, lateral mobility, relocation, compensation, and early identification of top performers.[9]

Schwartz suggests four requirements for clearing a path to the top for career-primary women: identifying them early, giving them the same opportunities for development that are offered to talented men in the organization, accepting them as valued members of the management team and listening to them, and recognizing that the business environment is more difficult and stressful for them than for their male peers.[10]

Since most of the work cited has been conducted in the business world, it might be suspected that universities and other educational organizations would be more sensitive to gender issues. My own observations and experience suggest that this is not the case, and detailed studies by the Ontario Council for the Status of Women have documented very tangibly that women have no greater access to senior positions in academia than anywhere else.

As Chair of the Royal Commission on Equality in Employment,[11]Canadian Judge Rosalie Abella asked, rhetorically, if universities, with their dedication to the advancement of learning and society could not provide leadership in the hiring of women to senior positions, then how could anyone expect private-sector corporations to do so? The surprising answer may be that economic necessity will win over social consciousness, and that corporations are outperforming universities in their adaptation to this new requirement.

One can only conclude this section by recognizing that all institutions, and notably universities, must and will appoint more women to senior management positions. While they should be given the same opportunities and support as men, it must also be recognized that they will bring different perspectives, skills and styles to the position, that their appointment will change the way some things are done, and that our organizations will be ultimately the better for this example of yet another more open approach to management.

The skills of leadership

Leadership is a lot more than charisma in these complex times. In fact, while personality and emotional leadership are important factors in the success of an organization's president, power based on charisma alone is, as Weber observed a long time ago,[12] temporary and, once it is lost, the stark contrast with the high expectations it initially creates is very disillusioning.

Instead, the modern manager must develop a wide range of skills to ensure that his or her decisions are soundly based and to the long-term benefit of the organization. Three key components of this leadership are strategic planning, institutional promotion and staff development, issues to which discussion now turns.

STRATEGIC PLANNING

No subject has received more attention over the past decade in the literature of organizational theory and development than strategic planning. Had this book been written about ten years ago, chances are it would be extolling the virtues of strategic planning through the creation of a special planning department within the corporation. This would have been staffed with specialist experts in all phases of corporate planning who would be charged with preparing all sorts of projections, plans and analyses to inform senior management decision-making.

However, experience with this approach has been less than satisfactory – too often, planning departments simply became large bureaucracies out of touch with the marketplace and with the corporate leadership itself. Corporate planners enjoyed a brief period of very high status, but disillusionment was not long in coming. Too often, strategic planning seemed like an academic exercise, imposed from above and directed by outside consultants, with very little immediate meaning for the busy managers who were supposed to help carry it out. Daniel Gray[13] describes a major aerospace and automotive supplier which, facing difficulties with its new emphasis on strategic planning, spent over $250,000 on a week-long conference of its top 40 managers during which consultants taught them strategic planning techniques in posh surroundings, with a last-day speech from the chief executive officer. For the fanfare, this initiative had very little ultimate impact on the organization.

For far too many companies, strategic planning was no more effective than were previous methods, but now they were saddled with large and expensive planning departments. As more and more chief executive officers realized this problem, massive cuts in planning departments followed. Strategic planning fell from favour as many Japanese companies, apparently without the same preoccupation, surpassed their American competitors in performance.[14]

However, the answer is surely not to fire all the planners, for organizations need excellent information and planning systems to succeed. On the contrary, as Michael Porter has observed, the time for strategic thinking has never been greater.

The solution is to improve strategic planning, not to abolish it.[15]

The trend more recently has been to involve line management throughout the strategic-planning process so that its issues are real, and planning is 'in touch' with what is going on in the organization and its surrounding milieu. Moreover, strategic planning must be closely tied to financial and systems planning (see Chapter 8) – if the strategic plan does not drive resource allocations, it becomes nothing more than a wish list, a 'pie-in-the-sky' dream about which most staff will quickly become cynical. Gray also notes the importance of linking information and reward systems to strategic planning.[16]

A 1984 *Business Week* cover story[17] assessed the results of earlier strategic plans of a number of American corporations, and found far more that were unsuccessful than successful. While it is difficult to draw broad conclusions from such a complex of factors, two stand out – the importance of involving line managers throughout the strategic planning process and the need for chief executive officers who are true strategic thinkers.[18]

Ultimately, strategic plans must be translated into operational plans which establish clear priorities, specific benchmarks and standards against which they can subsequently be evaluated and which direct allocations from the organizational budget. The operational plans will not only establish the power and credibility of the strategic plan, but will also force managers to establish priorities by not allowing them merely to live with pious platitudes, a situation which has so often been the result of strategic planning. As Hobbs and Heany point out, 'it appears to be much easier to conceive a new strategy than to carry it out.'[19]

Nor is it even enough to establish clear operating plans, for those responsible for steering them through an organization must follow through by ensuring their effective implementation and monitoring, on the basis of which the next plan should be determined. In this sense, strategic planning is never finished. Especially in a university, given academic freedom and its implied encouragement of dissent, it may be unrealistic to expect organization-wide commitment to all facets of a strategic plan. In some ways, the university climate offers advantages, for university leaders are more apt to be made aware of resistance and opposing viewpoints within their institutions than are their corporate counterparts who work in an environment which places a higher premium on company loyalty and compliance.

Perhaps a bigger internal danger to the success of strategic planning is apathy, with staff feeling little loyalty to or involvement with the dreams of their leaders. Indeed, Richardson has suggested that one of the major barriers to implementation is the perception of employees of a vast gap between their chief executive's rosy statements about the future and the reality in which most of them find themselves.[20]

My own experience with strategic planning has been an interesting one, in which most of the above lessons have been learned first-hand. Like most universities, Athabasca had a long-range plan which incorporated everyone's priorities into a general document which was strong on rhetoric but weak in establishing priorities or providing time-specific action plans for their realization. As vice-president academic, I was asked to come up with a strategic academic plan for the university for a five-year period which made specific and measurable the broad objectives of the long-range plan. In the traditional way of doing things at a university, I established and chaired a steering committee comprised of two deans of studies and three faculty members elected by the university's academic council (senate).

Using a technique called STOPS (an acronym for 'strengths', 'threats', 'opportunities', 'problems' and 'solutions'), the committee canvassed the university community for its identification of the key components of each of these factors facing the university at that point in its history. This process was very useful in ensuring broad consultation throughout the university environment and in increasing the visibility of the strategic-planning exercise. At the same time, it also raised expectations within the very diverse groupings that their particular agendas would be addressed as priority items. Concurrent with this internal exercise, several studies were commissioned to survey the external environment on similar issues and to identify major trends and concerns relevant to the university's future.

My attempts to oversee a democratic process, seeking consensus as to the major planks of the university's mission, mandate and planning, almost met with disaster. The three faculty members, as representatives of quite opposing viewpoints on such traditional left/right divisions as entrepreneurship versus social responsibility, and elitism versus openness, were clearly going to have difficulty agreeing on anything fundamental.

After months of position papers, debate and discussion, two of the three faculty members resigned (for different reasons), leaving the strategic-planning exercise in the lurch and me on a tightrope. The consultation process had gone as far as it could, and strong and immediate action was called for. With firm support from the president, I redefined the process so as to assign much more responsibility to the respective faculties and to give me the stronger position of making the final recommendations to the academic council and board of governors as vice-president academic, rather than as chair of a strategic-planning committee.

The resulting plan is a good one, with very specific priorities, indicators and timelines. It is measurable, ambitious and yet realistic; in fact, two years later, every major goal has thus far been achieved and some exceeded. What is of particular interest here is not its specifics, but the impact it has had on decision-making in the institution. It has shifted discussion away from what *ought* to be done to how it *will* be done; from dreaming to focused action. The dreaming does and must go on, but there is now a much greater tendency to carry the dreams forward into action plans, a process that is more and more common as more of the original plan is achieved. As dreams become realities, an institutional self-confidence develops, one that spawns even better ideas and new directions in response to changes in the environment.

It should not be surprising that the strategic-planning process deviated from its original design. While it would be folly to advocate the convoluted process which led to the creation of this particular plan, the experience underlines the importance of monitoring the process throughout and being quite open to change as new circumstances arise.

Of course, it is premature to judge the plan a successful one. The ultimate test of its worth will be not only in its successful implementation but also in results of that implementation which are in the best interests of the institution. In other words, the current process is far from over, and others in the organization are less buoyant about the plan than are those most closely associated with it. Some faculty feel that it is far too ambitious, especially given the levels of resources with which it is to be achieved; others are opposed to specific aspects; and still others are more concerned about issues it leaves out.

A fully committed executive team is absolutely essential to this process,[21] not only to ensure that the initial plans are well conceived, understood and supported throughout the organization, but also to oversee the long process of implementation, during which the plans will themselves be changing because of changes in the environment or levels of resources available. Ultimately, this concept of strategic planning becomes the value-driven management process advocated in this book. It calls for the chief executive officer and other members of the senior executive to be confident and highly visible advocates of the institutional vision and plans, but they must, at the same time, be sensitive to internal concerns and to environmental changes which may require the plans to be modified. It is a very large order, but also one which makes management a challenging and rewarding occupation.

A critical component of the process, and one that monitors its integrity, is strong institutional research. A major strength of Athabasca University's Strategic Academic Plan is its use of measurable 'benchmarks' in connection with almost all of its objectives. Hence, a target to increase completion rates by a specified figure by a specified date cannot be hedged or fudged, and can be measured by an independent observer. This builds accountability into the process, in terms both of setting the agenda for management to achieve over a certain time period and in judging their effectiveness in achieving that agenda. Where deadlines or targets are missed, the senior management will have explaining to do, leading to revisions in the plans or changes in the management itself.

Much of this strategic planning and follow-up implementation will take place in an atmosphere of 'crisis management'. Some textbooks leave the reader with the impression that a crisis is always precipitated by bad management. Certainly, a manager who is always operating in a state of crisis is probably someone who needs to do better planning or who lacks time-management or delegation skills. Nevertheless, while good 'anticipatory' management and planning can avoid such an atmosphere, which is often disruptive to the process, it is unrealistic to expect that any manager is so skilled or so in control of all factors that crisis can always be avoided. Moreover, many changes in the external environment or positions of competitors may not have been reasonably anticipated by even the best corporate leader. The real test of an effective manager is not the ability to avoid crisis, but to be able to take full advantage of it when it occurs.

An open and forthright response to crisis can overcome our natural tendency to resist change in times of strife. As Richardson asserts,[22] it is not a time for dissension among the institution's leaders; for, the time lost debating the most appropriate response may be critical to the success of the plan, any plan. Good communications and strong leadership can capitalize on a crisis, one advantage of which is that people are less apt to question the need for change, and hence energy can be directed at the problem of what kind of change, instead of whether change is needed at all. This is not to support the all-too-familiar tactic of 'creating' a crisis to serve one's own ends. While this tactic may be justifiable on occasion, it ultimately produces the same result as that encountered by the boy who cried 'Wolf!' once too often.

Strategic planning, then, is still the best answer to the need for clear and integrated leadership in today's institutions. No institution should provide more evidence of being a 'learning institution' than a university, and, if we accept De Geus's notion of 'planning as learning',[23] we will understand the role of strategic planning as the value-driven leadership mechanism which is essential to our future success.

> We understand that the only competitive advantage the company of the future will have is its managers' ability to learn faster than their competitors. So the companies that succeed will be those that continually nudge their managers towards revising their views of the world. The challenges for the planner are considerable. So are the rewards.[24]

Only through effective strategic planning and management will universities successfully cope with the discontinuous change which they increasingly face today.[25]

Institutional marketing

Universities have long resisted attempts by administrators to import and impose concepts and terms from the business world. Indeed, until very recently, many denied the legitimate place of business schools within their concept of a university (the demand for places in such programmes has tended to break down this resistance, especially where the universities have had to fight to maintain their student enrolments).

Increasingly, however, as they enter a more competitive environment and one of increasing public accountability, universities have had to pay attention to such concerns as 'their image', promotion and marketing. Far too frequently, this is not attempted until a crisis point, usually when falling enrolments are seriously undermining the institution's fiscal position. Again, too often, attempts to develop a marketing plan expose the lack of clear mission statements and strategic plans, and what starts out as a 'simple' marketing exercise ends up turning the institution upside down as staff agonize over its priorities in trying to come to terms with the messages it really wants to send out.

A particular concern for open universities is the danger that its marketing campaigns will breed false expectations among its students. It is inevitable that institutions which offer open admissions and flexible scheduling attract some students looking for the easy way through. However, anyone who has secured a degree through correspondence, distance education or other forms of off-campus and part-time learning knows that it is a very demanding way to pursue an education. As noted earlier (Chapter 6, pp 85–7), it makes unusual demands on the student's study and time-management skills and on his or her persistence.

Nevertheless, the 'competitive advantage' of an open-learning institution is its accessibility and the flexibility it offers to the part-time adult learner. It is therefore not surprising that such institutions regularly promote these attributes, stressing the ease of admissions, the immediacy with which students can start and the flexibility of timetables and choices of delivery systems. By emphasizing access, convenience and flexibility, such promotions can further build on common (and false) perceptions that this is an easier way to get an education.

Herein lies a dilemma. One can hardly expect open-learning institutions to boast, 'There's no more difficult way to get a degree!' or 'Chances are, you'll drop out before you complete this programme!' but the reality is that far too many first-time students totally underestimate the demands of open-learning systems and drop out as a result. As discussed in Chapter 6, the answer lies primarily in the institution's 'pre-admissions' and orientation services rather than in any change in its marketing.

The vagueness of such concepts as 'open learning' and 'distance education' poses another marketing challenge. At a time when promotion and fund-raising are so critical to an institution's success, how does one explain these concepts concisely and effectively? The preferred approach may be to avoid all the details of these complex terms, and simply promote the advantages the institution offers to the student – a university that tailors its services to the needs of the individual and that gives opportunity to those lacking formal qualifications, or second chances to those who have not succeeded in earlier attempts.

While it may be more difficult to explain, the concept of an open university has one invaluable advantage – it is very different from the norm. It can thus be seen as a 'new message', one that is very welcome to many who have been critical of universities in the past. Those who view higher-educational institutions as elitist, unresponsive ivory towers will be very open to open-learning institutions, which are working so hard to break down the barriers to a university education that have existed for so long.

It is not easy to describe and 'explain' an open university to someone without previous exposure to it. Prevailing negative attitudes towards 'correspondence' education, open admissions and part-time students can lead to serious questioning of the status and academic credibility of such institutions. The time is past, however, when open-university staff need feel defensive about their institutions, which have not only dramatically increased accessibility to higher education but have demonstrated that many more people can be successful in universities than had ever previously been anticipated, and that there are real economic and social benefits for societies which open up higher education in this way. There is no question in my mind that this is the 'right business' to be in today, and that the open university will not only increasingly find its niche, but also provide leadership in defining the university of the future.

At a time when institutional fund-raising is so critical, open universities have the advantage of establishing their own distinct market niche, one that separates them clearly from most institutions of higher learning. Applying Michael Porter's work to distance education, Murgatroyd and Woudstra note the importance of selecting among his three market strategies (excellent provider, least-cost provider, or only provider of a learning experience for a particular niche), each of which will require a different approach to management if it is to be successful.[26]

There is, however, another dimension to marketing which has posed more difficulties for open-learning institutions – their need for acceptance and credibility among the rest of the higher-education sector. This has not been easy, especially in countries like Germany and Japan where the university tradition has tended most strongly to elitism. In this context, the recognition and prominence which Britain's Open University has achieved in only 20 years has done a great deal for other open-learning institutions. While there has been a price for this, in the form of conservative pressures on such institutions to be less radical than they might otherwise be (see discussion in Chapter 4), a countervailing benefit is the influence of open universities on their more traditional counterparts and the latter's increasing acceptance of such notions as distance education, interinstitutional accreditation and more open admissions for adult students.

As might be expected, given the earlier sections on systems development and strategic planning, the position taken here is that institutional marketing follows naturally from a well-designed strategic plan which defines the institution's mission, priorities and target student groups. Again, it is not a task that can be left to public-relations specialists, but it is one that is central to the effectiveness of the institution's leadership group.

Staff development

If hiring decisions are the most important factors in the success of an organization, how it treats and develops its existing staff must be next on the priority list. Just as many executive officers pay too little attention to their hiring processes, so they ignore or underrate the importance of staff development. There is considerable irony in this. In some ways, universities pay a lot more attention to staff development than do most other institutions. They give faculty members a great deal of autonomy and unallocated time, encourage them to pursue their own research and scholarly interests, support research projects, fund travel to conferences, and encourage them to publish their ideas and findings. There is generous provision for sabbatical leaves and hence an inbuilt recognition that staff must keep up-to-date in their field and ideas.

On the other hand, many universities are carrying these out in a rather rote fashion, paying far too little attention to the value and fundamental importance of continuing staff development. Sabbaticals, professional-development leave and research are traditional, almost ritualistic benefits, and there is often very little scrutiny of what is actually being done. There is still too little accountability in the sense that one can do a great deal or very little during a leave or sabbatical without response from the institution. Staff development is thus left largely to the individual, without reference to the mission or specific goals of the institution or department.

Moreover, there is often a large gap between support for faculty members and that for other members of staff at the institution, a practice which can undermine the effectiveness of the whole programme by ignoring the importance of other professional and support staff in the realization of the academic programme. This is particularly the case in an open university where, very often, students have more contact with tutors and other professional and support staff than they do with the academic faculty. The lack of effective orientation and development programmes for the part-time tutors who interact directly with students on a regular basis is a serious weakness in many of our open universities.

These practices (or lack of them) contrast quite vividly with those in our most successful corporations, especially those in quickly developing technological areas, where there is a tremendous emphasis on staff development – on-the-job training and upgrading, educational programmes (both within the institution and support for those pursuing it elsewhere), conference attendance, and similar programming. The difference is that corporations tend to be more systematic and integrated in their approaches to staff development, linking these approaches closely to their strategic plans and market competition.

Even when there is a formal staff development programme in an educational institution, it too often takes the form of high-profile courses, seminars and 'one-shot' offerings quite transparently intended to change staff in specific ways. The low success rates of such endeavours are well portrayed by Smyth,[27] who sees the villain as the politicization and centralization of education that robs teachers of their creativity and initiative.

The answer is not necessarily to abandon traditional university practices, for, academic freedom, in its best sense, is a protection against undue administrative interference in research and scholarship, but to build on existing practices. The large investment of public funds in universities brings with it an accountability as to how these funds are spent. There should be no doubt that the very nature of a university, as an institution devoted to the development and communication of new ideas, requires that it be a leader in ongoing staff development. This should be even more the case in an open university, with its dedication to lifelong learning. In all cases, however, the foundation must be respect for the integrity and professional competence of the individual staff member, and programmes which both support and challenge academics as they wrestle with the complexities of educating themselves and others.

Summary: leadership and integrity in the management of open learning

The central message of this book has been that those responsible for the management of open learning must learn to be more open managers and to lead organizations which are 'learning' organizations. I believe that there is a great deal to be learned from the management of open universities, and that there are important lessons for education, for organizations and for leadership to be derived from this experience.

EDUCATION

The world's open universities have already justified their commitment to open admissions through the number and success of their graduates who would not otherwise have had access to postsecondary education. They have provided leadership in instructional design, in flexibility and adaptability, in student-support services and in training models which have had considerable impact on conventional institutions and which are modifying prevailing attitudes about the learning systems of the future. They have been less successful in their adaptation of new technologies to learning systems, but there is evidence that they will be more successful in this domain in the future. They are increasingly cost-efficient, especially in developing countries, where they can serve an enormous clientele at very little relative cost.

The past decade has seen a realization of their potential, to the extent that their place in the world of higher education is firmly established. It is my own view that they will continue to be successful, so successful, in fact, that distinctions between 'conventional' and 'open' universities will gradually disappear as more and more institutions adopt and adapt the structures and processes of distance education and open learning in responding to the needs of society and their students.

ORGANIZATIONAL THEORY

The professional/bureaucratic conflict outlined in Chapter 2 is nowhere more evident than in an open university, which combines an industrial course-production model with academia. As organizations which must constantly change in response to societal needs, open universities must avoid institutionalizing open learning so that it becomes a new rigidity in itself. It is easy to observe processes of conservatism at institutions like Athasbasca University and Britain's Open University, and one real test of the leadership of such institutions will be their ability constantly to challenge and change the way they do things. Only if they are successful will they be the 'learning' organizations that they purport to be, and continue to provide models and case studies for the development of organizational theory and for the emulation of even private-sector institutions in the 'knowledge' society.

MANAGEMENT AND LEADERSHIP

The argument has been advanced that the successful development of open universities requires 'open management', a value-driven approach which encompasses the qualities of open learning – openness, flexibility and a strong commitment not only to universal educational opportunity but also to the support systems requisite for student success.

Above all, the success of open universities depends on leadership and vision – a value-driven commitment to the ideals of open learning, honesty and integrity without rigidity – a flexible approach in a world of ambiguity, change and challenge. If every institutional leader strives for open management, leadership which encompasses the values of open learning which we hold up for our students, the world's open universities will be much more effective institutions and will increasingly be seen as models for the university of tomorrow.

Notes

1. Peters, T (1988), *Thriving on Chaos: Handbook for a Management Revolution,* New York: Alfred A Knopf, p 45.
2. Morrison, T R (1989), 'Beyond Legitimacy: Facing the Future in Distance Education', *International Journal of Lifelong Education,* 6 (1), Jan–March, p 13.
3. Weber, M (1947), *The Theory of Social and Economic Organization,* ed with introduction by Parsons, T, New York: Free Press, pp 64 ff.
4. Adler, N J and Izraeli, D N (1988), *Women in Management Worldwide,* Armouk, New York: M E Sharpe.
5. Davidson, M and Cooper, C (1984), *She Needs a Wife: Problems of Women Managers,* Bradford: MCB University Press, pp 12–13.
6. Ibid, p 18.
7. Ibid, pp 17, 21.
8. Schwartz, F (1989), 'Management Women and the New Facts of Life', *Harvard Business Review,* 67 (1), Jan–Feb, p 68.
9. Ibid, p 66.
10. Ibid, p 70.
11. Abella, R S (1984), 'Equality in Employment: A Royal Commission Report', *Report of the Commission on Equality in Employment,* Ottawa: Government of Canada.
12. Weber, M, op cit, pp 64 ff.
13. Gray, D H (1986), 'Uses and Misuses of Strategic Planning', *Harvard Business Review,* 64 (1), Jan–Feb, pp 91–2.
14. Porter, M (1987), 'Corporate Strategy: the State of Strategic Thinking', *The Economist,* 23 May, p 17.

15. Ibid, p 18.
16. Gray, op cit, p 96.
17. 'The New Breed of Strategic Planner' (1984), *Business Week,* 17 Sept, pp 62–7.
18. Ibid.
19. Hobbs, J M and Heany, D F (1977), 'Coupling Strategy to Operating Plans', *Harvard Business Review,* 55 (3), May–June, p 119.
20. Richardson, P (1986), 'The Challenge of Strategic Change', *Canadian Business Review,* Autumn, p 30.
21. Ibid, p 31.
22. Ibid.
23. De Geus, A P (1988), 'Planning as Learning', *Harvard Business Review,* 66 (2), March–April, pp 70–4.
24. Ibid, p 74.
25. For further discussion of this point, see Murgatroyd, S and Woudstra, A (1989), 'Issues in the Management of Distance Education', *American Journal of Distance Education,* 3 (1), pp 4–19.
26. Ibid, pp 12–13.
27. Smyth, J (1989), 'When Teachers Theorize Their Practice', in Evans, T and Nation, D (eds), *Critical Reflections in Distance Education,* London: Falmer Press, pp 209–10.

Glossary of Terms

AU	Athabasca University
ACCESS	Alberta educational broadcasting agency
AGT	Alberta Government Telephones
AI	Artificial intelligence
AT & T	American Telegraph and Telephone
AERA	American Educational Research Association
ASPESA	Australian & South Pacific External Studies Association
CADE	Canadian Association of Distance Education
CDLDC	Canadian Distance Learning Development Centre
CSSE	Canadian Society for Studies in Education
CEGEP	College d'enseignement general et professionel
EADTU	European Association of Distance Teaching Universities
e-mail	Electronic mail
ICDE	International Council for Distance Education
ISDN	Integrated services digital network (fax, e-mail etc)
IT	Information Technology
MIT	Massachusetts Institute of Technology
OU	Open University (of the United Kingdom unless otherwise indicated)
STOPS	'Strengths, threats, opportunities, problems, solutions' process
VDT	Visual display terminal
UKOU	Open University of the United Kingdom
WCCUDE	Western Canadian Council on University Distance Education

Bibliography

Abrioux, D, Paul, R, Shale, D, and Thomas, D (1984). 'Non-Traditional Education and Organizational Change: The Case of Athabasca University', paper presented at the AERA/ASHE Conference, San Francisco, 28 Oct.

Adler, N J and Izraeli, D N (1988). *Women in Management Worldwide.* Armouk, NY: M E Sharpe.

Badaracco, J L and Ellsworth, R R (1989). *Leadership and the Quest for Integrity.* Boston: Harvard Business School Press.

Bagley, B and Challis, B (1985). *Inside Open Learning.* Coombe Lodge, Bristol: The Further Education Staff College.

Baldridge, J V (1971). *Power and Conflict in the University: Research in the Sociology of Complex Organizations.* New York: John Wiley and Sons.

Bellini, J (1986). *High Tech Holocaust.* San Francisco: Sierra Club Books.

Bennis, W and Nanus, B (1985). *Leaders: The Strategies for Taking Charge.* New York: Harper & Row.

Birch, D and Latcham, J (1984). *Managing Open Learning.* Coombe Lodge, Bristol: The Further Education Staff College.

Boud, E (ed) (1988). *Developing Student Autonomy in Learning.* London: Kogan Page.

Bradford, D L and Cohen, A R (1984). *Managing for Excellence: The Guide to Developing High Performance in Contemporary Organizations:* New York: John Wiley & Sons.

Brooke, M Z (1984). *Centralization and Autonomy: A Study in Organizational Behaviour.* London: Holt, Rinehart & Winston.

Brookfield, S (1982). Independent learners and correspondence students. *Teaching at a Distance, 22,* 26–33.

(1987). *Developing Critical Thinking: Challenging Adults to Explore Alternative Ways of Thinking and Acting.* Milton Keynes,

England: Open University Press.

Burge, E. (1988). Beyond andragogy: Some explorations for distance learning design. *Journal of Distance Education* **3** (1), 5–23.

Burrell, G and Morgan, G (1979). *Sociological Paradigms and Organisational Analysis.* London: Heinemann.

Butts, R F (1955). *A Cultural History of Western Education: Its Social and Intellectual Foundations.* New York: McGraw-Hill.

Callan, P M (ed) (1986). *Environmental Scanning for Strategic Leadership.* San Francisco: Jossey-Bass.

Chang, T M et al, (1983). *Distance Learning: On the Design of an Open University.* Boston: Kluwer-Nijhoff Publishing.

Chesterton, P (1985). Curriculum control in distance education. *Teaching at a Distance,* **1** (26), 32.

Cohen, M D and March, J G (1974). *Leadership and Ambiguity.* New York: McGraw-Hill.

Daniel, J S and Marquis, C (1979). Interaction and independence: Getting the mixture right. *Teaching at a Distance,* **14,** 29–44.

Daniel, J S, Stroud, M R and Thompson, J A (eds) (1982). *Learning at a Distance: A World Perspective.* Edmonton: Athabasca University.

Davidson, M J and Cooper, C L (1984). *She Needs a Wife: Problems of Women Managers.* Bradford, England: MCB University Press Ltd.

De Geus, A P (1988). Planning as learning. *Harvard Business Review,* **66** (2), March–April, 70–4.

Drucker, P (1985). *Innovation and Entrepreneurship: Practice and Principles.* New York: Harper & Row.

Escotet, M (1980). Adverse factors in the development of an open university in Latin America. *Programme Learning and Educational Technology,* **17** (4), Nov, 262–70.

Eurich, N P (1985). *Corporate Classrooms: The Learning Business.* Princeton, N J: The Carnegie Foundation for the Advancement of Teaching.

Evans, T and Nation, D (eds) (1989). *Critical Reflections on Distance Education.* London: The Falmer Press.

Fage, J and Mills, R (1986). Student–tutor feedback in the open university. *Open Learning,* **1** (3), 44–6.

Faith, K (1988). Gender as an issue in distance education. *Journal of Distance Education,* III (1), spring, 75–9.

Farnes, N (1976). An educational technologist looks at student-centred learning. *British Journal of Educational Technology,* **7** (1), 61–4.

Fletcher, B (1968). *Universities in the Modern World.* London: Pergamon Press.

Friere, P (1970). *Pedagogy of the Oppressed.* New York: Continuum.

Gibbs, G (1981). *Teaching Students to Learn: A Student-Centred*

Approach. Milton Keynes, England: Open University Press.

Gray, D H (1986). Uses and misuses of strategic planning. *Harvard Business Review,* **64** (1), Jan–Feb, 91–2.

Grimwade, J (1985). *Proceedings of the Thirteenth World Conference* (microfiche). Melbourne: ICDE.

Handy, C (1989). *The Age of Unreason.* London: Business Books.

    (1985). *Understanding Organizations,* Third Edition. Harmondsworth, Middlesex: Penguin Books.

Harris, D (1987). *Openness and Closure in Distance Education,* Lewes, England: The Falmer Press.

    (1988). The micro-politics of openness. *Open Learning,* **3** (2), June, 13–16.

Henderson, E S and Nathenson, M B (eds) (1984). *Independent Learning in Higher Education.* Englewood Cliffs, N J: Educational Technology Publications.

Hickman, C R and Silva, M A (1984). *Creating Excellence: Managing Corporate Culture, Strategy and Change in the New Age.* New York: New American Library.

Hobbs, J M and Heany, D F (1977). Coupling strategy to operating plans. *Harvard Business Review,* **55** (3), May–June, 119–26.

Hodgson, V E et al (eds) (1987). *Beyond Distance Teaching – Towards Open Learning.* Milton Keynes, England: The Open University Press.

Illich, I (1971). *Deschooling Society.* New York: Harper & Row.

Inglis, P (1989). Supporting learning at a distance: External students' perceptions of the contribution and importance of certain teaching and learning conditions to their development of learning independence, with particular reference to the affective domain. Unpublished thesis submitted in partial fulfilment of the doctor of philosophy degree, University of Queensland, Australia.

Kandel, I L (1933). *Comparative Education.* Cambridge, Mass: Riverside Press.

Kaye, A and Rumble, G (1981). *Distance Teaching for Higher and Adult Education.* London: Croom Helm & Open University Press.

Knowles, M (1973). *Self-Directed Learning: A Guide for Learners and Teachers.* New York: Association Press.

Kouzes, J M and Posner, B Z (1987). *The Leadership Challenge.* San Francisco: Jossey-Bass.

Krajnc, A (1988). Social isolation and learning effectiveness in distance education. *Ziff Papiere 71,* Hagen: Fernuniversität.

Lewis, R (1986). What is open learning? *Open Learning,* **1** (2), 5–10.

    (1990). Open learning and the misuse of language: A response to Greville Rumble. Open Learning, **4** (3), Feb.

Lewis, R and Spencer, D (1986). *What is Open Learning?* London: Council for Educational Technology.

Marriot, S (1981). *A Backstairs to a Degree: Demands for an Open University in Late Victorian England.* Leeds, England: Leeds Studies in Adult and Continuing Education.

Masson, J P (1987). La clientèle étudiante et les institutions de formation à distance. *Journal of Distance Education,* 2 (fall), 55–64.

Merton, R K et al (1952). *Reader in Bureaucracy.* Glencoe, Illinois: Free Press.

Millard, J (1985). Local tutor–student contact in the open university. *Teaching at a Distance,* 26, 11–22.

Millet, J D (1962). *The Academic Community: An Essay on Organization.* New York: McGraw-Hill.

    (1980). *Managing Governance and Leadership.* New York: AMACOM.

Mintzberg, H (1989). *Mintzberg on Management: Inside Our Strange World of Organizations.* New York: Free Press.

Moore, M (1986). Self-directed learning and distance education. *Journal of Distance Education,* 1 (1), 7–24.

Morgan, A (1985). What shall we do about independent learning? *Teaching at a Distance,* 26, 38–45.

Morrison, T R (1989). Beyond legitimacy: Facing the future in distance education. *International Journal of Lifelong Education,* 6 (1), Jan–March, 3–24.

Mugridge, I and Kaufman, D (eds) (1986). *Distance Education in Canada.* London: Croom Helm.

Murgatroyd, S and Woudstra, A (1989). Issues in the management of distance education. *American Journal of Distance Education,* 3 (1), 4–19.

Neil, M W (ed) (1981). *Education of Adults at a Distance.* London: Kogan Page.

The new breed of strategic planner. (1984). *Business Week,* 17 Sept, 62–7.

Osterman, P (ed) (1983). *Employment Policies of Large Firms,* New York: MIT Press.

Paine, N (ed) (1988). *Open Learning in Transition: An Agenda for Action.* Cambridge: National Extension College.

Parsons, T (1951). *The Social System.* Glencoe, Illinois: Free Press.

Paul, R H (1986). Access to failure? The challenge of open education at Athabasca University. *Community Services Catalyst,* XVI (2), 18–22.

    (1989). Is the Open Door a Revolving Door? A Plea for Stronger Student Support in Distance Education. Paper presented at ETIC '89, Birmingham, England, April (to be published in conference proceedings).

(1989). Lessons from Collaboration in Distance Education in Western Canada. Paper presented at Recent Trends in Adult Education, Centre for Canadian Studies, Queen's University, Belfast, May (to be published in conference proceedings).

(1989). The management of open learning. *Aurora Magazine,* Athabasca University, Spring/Summer, pp 31–2.

(1990). Towards a new measure of success: Developing independent learners. *Open Learning* (Feb), 37–44.

(1990). The Integration and Management of Information Technology in Distance Education. Paper to be presented at the World Congress of ICDE, Caracas, Venezuela, Nov.

Perry, W (1976). *Open University: A Personal Account.* Milton Keynes, England: Open University Press.

Peters, T (1988). *Thriving on Chaos: Handbook for a Management Revolution.* New York: Alfred A Knopf.

Peters, T and Austin, N (1985). *A Passion for Excellence: The Leadership Difference.* New York: Random House.

Piercy, N (ed) (1984). *The Management Implications of New Information Technology.* London: Croom Helm.

Porter, M (1987). Corporate strategy: The state of strategic thinking. *The Economist,* 23 May, 17.

Quinn, J B, Mintzberg, H and James, R M (1988). *Strategy Process.* Englewood Cliffs, N J: Prentice-Hall.

Richardson, P (1986). The challenge of strategic change. *Canadian Business Review,* autumn, 29–32.

Robinson, N (1965). Principal and Teacher Supervisory Relationships: Problems and Perspectives. Alberta Leadership Course, Edmonton, pp 55–61.

Rockart, J (1988). The line takes the leadership – IS Management in a wired society. *Sloan Management Review,* (summer), 57–64.

Rumble, G (1989). 'Open Learning', 'distance learning', and the misuse of language. *Open Learning* (June), 32–40.

(1986). *The Planning and Management of Distance Education.* London: Croom Helm.

Rumble, G and Harry, K (1986). *The Distance Teaching Universities.* London: Croom Helm.

Ryans, C C and Shanklin, W L (1986). *Strategic Planning, Marketing and Public Relations, and Fund-Raising in Higher Education.* Metuchen, N J: Scarecrow Press.

Schwartz, F (1989). Management women and the new facts of life. *Harvard Business Review,* **67** (1), Jan–Feb, 68.

Sewart, D and Daniel, J S (eds) (1988). *Developing Distance Education. D and Holmberg, B (eds) (1982). Distance Educaal Perspectives.* London: Croom Helm.

Shute, A G et al (1986). Teletraining in the corporate environment. Cincinatti, Ohio: Sales and Marketing Education Division, AT & T.

Silverman, D (1970). *The Theory of Organisations: A Sociological Framework.* London: Heinemann.

Simerly, R G et al (1987). *Strategic Planning and Leadership in Continuing Education.* San Francisco: Jossey-Bass.

Smith, K (1984). *Diversity Down Under.* Toowoomba, Queensland: Darling Downs Institute Press.

Smith, P and Kelly, M (eds) (1987). *Distance Education and the Mainstream.* London: Croom Helm.

Smyth, J (1989). When teachers theorize their practice: a reflexive approach to a distance education course. In: Evans, T and Nation, D, op cit, pp 197–233.

Strategic Planning Group (1988). A strategic educational plan for the Canadian Distance Learning Development Centre. Athabasca University, April.

Stroup, H (1966). *Bureaucracy in Higher Education.* New York: Free Press.

Sweet, R (ed) (1989). *Post-Secondary Distance Education in Canada: Policies, Practices and Priorities.* Athabasca: Athabasca University and Canadian Society for Studies in Education.

Tait, A (1989). Democracy and distance education: The role of tutorial and counselling services. *Journal of Distance Education,* 3 (1), 95–9.

Tait, A (ed) (1989). *Interaction and Independence: Student Support in Distance Education and Open Learning,* conference papers for the ICDE/UKOU Conference at Downing College, Cambridge, Sept 19–22.

Thorpe, M (1979). When is a course not a course? *Teaching at a Distance,* **16,** 13–18.

Thorpe, M and Grugeon, D (1987). *Open Learning for Adults.* London: Longman.

Tight, M (ed), (1983). *Adult Learning and Education,* London: Croom Helm.

von Prummer, C and Rossie, U (1988). Gender in distance education at the Fernuniversität. *Open Learning,* 3 (2), June, 3–12.

Weber, M (1947). *The Theory of Social and Economic Organizations.* Trans, Henderson A M and Parsons T. Ed with an introd by Parsons T. New York: Oxford University Press.

Wickett, R (1986). Models for independent learning: Applications for distance education. *Open Campus,* **12,** 27–33.

Wolfe, R and Murgatroyd, S (1979). The open university and the negotiation of knowledge. *Higher Education Review,* **11** (2), 9–16.

Name Index

Subject Index